Katie

Oceans of love

Tana
xxx

Making Waves

MUSINGS, REFLECTIONS
& INSPIRATION

Awaken the Light Within

IONA RUSSELL

 That Guy's House

ISBN - 978-1-913479-06-0 (print)

ISBN - 978-1-913479-03-9 (ebook)

Book Design by Michael Maloney

Cover Artwork by Michelle St.Onge

First edition published in 2020

That Guy's House
20-22 Wenlock Road
London
England
N1 7GU

www.ThatGuysHouse.com

Dedication

Mum, thank you for your unconditional support on my journey in this lifetime. You taught me what it means to live from the Heart and to embody grace, compassion and integrity with humour. I know you are with me always in Spirit. I love you.

To my son, I am so proud of the teacher you are to me. I thank you for the lessons, laughter and spirit that you bring to our lives. You make me want to be a better BEing. From the days of imaginary games, teaching yourself to ride a bike, and navigating your own path—you inspire me.

Contents

Introduction

Tears at Midnight

You know you've hit another rock bottom when you sit up in bed, crying through snotty tears, "I can't do this! I can't live like this any longer!" I was lying in bed next to my then husband, where we lived in Texas. We'd emigrated there from Edinburgh, Scotland after getting married, with my seven-year-old son. To all onlookers, it appeared like I was living the American dream minus the pool.

We had the international holidays, cars, motorbikes (yes, I had a bike, too), and friends. We went to live gigs, went sailing, and toasted marshmallows at the top of a live volcano in Guatemala. Life appeared full.

What was it I couldn't do?

On the inside, however, I was crying out to be saved, to be happy, to find joy and find my purpose. I just hadn't realised at this point that I had to save myself.

The buck stops and starts with yourself. I'd tried looking for satisfaction in food, drink, drugs, overworking, over-exercising and undervaluing myself with inflated expectations of who I should be. In fact, I'd basically spent my entire life searching outside myself for happiness, wholeness, love and joy. I didn't know yet that all this and more was already there inside me.

What was it couldn't do?

I thought it was live in Texas.

I thought if we just moved back to Edinburgh, I would be ok.

I thought if we just moved to California, I would be happy.

But happiness is an inside job, and I was about to learn that.

My thoughts were keeping me stuck.

I was keeping me stuck unhappy like an outdated needle on an old record player, and I was stuck repeating the same groove.

I had to change!

I was put onto antidepressants for the 4th time, which did their thing to get me motivated and out of my icky funk, as well as brave enough to start on my path to finding myself.

Do you know what the biggest game changer was? It's so simple.

I got quiet; I got my Zen on with meditation!! I became "Zen Iona."

Meditation actually saved my life. Cue the song, "Last night a DJ (meditation) saved my life . . ." It was in surrendering, when I "Let Go, Let

God" that I found the connection I'd been searching for outside myself. It was there all along, hidden in plain sight.

Now, before you get all tense at the word "God," just relax. Call this essence whatever you want—the Source of Universal Love, Mother Earth, Gaia, Your Higher Self, The Divine, The Great Oneness, Universe has your back, Buddha, Gaia, Goddess, Your inner light, Wizard of Oz or Bob. To me, all roads lead to Rome, so name your own road.

*   *   *

Meditation is listening—quieting the mind so that then, you hear the whispers of the Soul on the breeze, dancing across the ocean of infinite possibilities.

Now, I utterly sucked at both (Surrender and Meditation). I'm not saying I had that "Hallelujah" moment . . . it was subtle and I was NOW desperate. I felt there had to be something "more," and I was ready for it!

As a rebellious teenager, however, I boycotted structured spiritual Practises, running away from my hippie parents and their Buddhist paths. I'd been raised on a farm in the hills of Wales with FREEDOM, goats, hens and horses. I now thank them for giving me such a strong foundation in thinking outside the box in terms of spirituality, humanity, compassion and unconditional love.

We weren't your average family farm. We had a Shrine room, a wooden Gompa (a hut built for silent meditation) and Buddhist monks in full burgundy robes visiting along with the sixteenth Karmapa, the spiritual leader of the Karma Kagyu lineage of Tibetan Buddhism.

I knew we were different, and I didn't like it.

I ran the other way into the arms of superficial/false salvation—self-sabotage and self-destruction, using alcohol, food and drugs to fill the void in my soul. I had some fun (so much FUN), but I was left hungry and dissatisfied. I'd been looking outside myself for all the resources I craved—in approval from others, my peer group, drink, drugs, partying, being loud and the centre of attention and even travelling to go find myself.

I'd been there all along—as are you, there inside at your authentic core, your Soul SELF as One with the Universe. Knowing this (at your core) will save you decades of searching. You're welcome.

This sense I had of being lost, restless and unfulfilled meant that my fears kept me stuck. My beliefs and fears of being judged as not enough, along with shame, guilt and unworthiness manifested as depression, anxiety, bulimia, addiction, lack of confidence and lack of self-belief.

Silently screaming from the inside, I knew without a shadow of a doubt that I had to calm the waters of my soul.

Coincidentally (this is the Universe winking and giving you confirmation or a nudge in the right direction), I stumbled across Madhavi Kata Chalasani, an amazing BEautiful Energy Medicine and Shamanic Healer at Chakra Bliss Center. She ran a non-denominational meditation group and I felt magnetically drawn to her. We don't need to look at the why or the how; just trust, have faith and fall forwards. I've no idea how I found her or what drew me to her, but she inspired me and led me back to myself.

The path started with Meditation and led me to a remembering, awakening and awareness of my Soul Medicine gifts. Along the way, I embraced Energy Healing, Ancestral Lineage Clearing, Chinese medicine, Chakra Vibrations, Oracle cards, Heart Healing, Starseeds, Lightworkers, Goddesses, Quantum Physics, Quantum field healing and Integrative Health—to name a few of the areas that interested me—plus my own gifts, of course.

"Change the Way You Look At Things, and the Things You Look At Change"

Wayne Dyer

I became inspired through meditation, and it felt SOOOO GOOOD. I had to continue with MORE of this. It became an integral part of my life and not a "thing" I had to do. My husband at the time referred to my transformation as "Zen Iona." I became calmer and a much less shouty mum. I found inner peace and wasn't triggered as much by other peoples' actions like I'd been before. This is how "Zen Iona" and my true calling for helping others came into being.

The truth, however, is that I've always wanted to help others. I just didn't know when I was younger that it was my calling, my passion. It simply came naturally. When I was a child, I'm told I played with the kids excluded by others. I volunteered with the Citizens Advice Bureau (CAB) in the UK, assisting those without a voice or without the financial circumstances to seek the legal advice they needed. I specialised in homelessness and Social Benefits appeals. I've been the executive of a charitable grant giving trust in Scotland, helping the community and organisations that wouldn't receive funding otherwise. I worked as a Court Appointed Special Advocate (CASA), representing the best interests of children removed by social services in Texas. It broke my heart that such work was needed, but I loved the work itself.

I have the heart of a Dragon in fighting for all those in my care. I once flew out of state with my then husband's blessing to review a placement that wouldn't have been funded otherwise. We put the expenses on our credit card. When you are inspired, you go above and beyond the call of duty.

The one thing that stays true throughout these callings is that I have always believed that no matter who you are, where you are from or your personal circumstances, you can change. I couldn't change the system, but I could change the hearts and souls of those I worked with.

It is my purpose to help ignite the hearts and minds of all people who want to create change and transform their lives, finding their Soul Purpose so that they can awaken their unique gifts. Know this: It is possible to reinvent yourself from the inside out and live the Life you were born to live—your BEST life.

My journey back home to myself, to BEing whole and complete as One with the Universe, meant looking at the world through a fresh lens. For a long time, what was missing for me was a true cheerleader and challenger of the soulful kind to guide me on my voyage to aligning my mind/body/spirit. I hope to be that cheerleader for you through the pages of this book. It contains quotes and inspiration that were part of my journey and are part of the processes that I use with my clients today.

We're either living in Fear or Love, and when we aren't living from a place of love, we are calling for Love. We all have innate wellbeing, health and happiness within us. We've just forgotten. We've forgotten who we were before "they" told us who to be. Before we told ourselves how to be. Before we put on the Mask of conformity and hid behind it. We can choose to transform our lives by "ReBooting" ourselves to who we are at our core on a Soul level, back to our authentic Self. Remembering who we are—the wild and gifted wise wo(man), soul siSTAR—a Spiritual being having a human experience. It's time for you to Shine Bright and BE Magnificent!

*There are BONUS materials available on my website for you to download, including meditations, PDF's, journal prompts and more. I will continue to add to this over time as I am inspired to create more.
 https://ionarussell.com/making-waves-bonus-material/

How to use this book

This book contains **musings, reflections and inspiration** that have worked for me and my clients on the quest to uncover and awaken the light within, to embrace who we were born to be.

I invite you to dip in and out of these pages as you are drawn to. You can either follow along in a linear fashion or intuitively flip through the pages as you're guided where to stop. I trust that the insight you receive that day will be appropriate for you.

Please implement the quotes, affirmations, techniques and suggested "Peaceful Practises" in whatever way you wish to create your own Daily Practise. A daily Practise can change; it doesn't have to be methodically repeated. It consists of moments that you set aside for you. Some of these Practises may just become a part of your life over time.

You'll discover:

Meditations
Intention-setting
Gratitude
Movement
Creativity
Goals with Soul
Walks in Nature
Prayer
Chakra Clearing

Hawaiian Philosophies
Ho'oponopono
Developing a Morning Routine
Tuning into Inner Wisdom
Personal Peaceful Practises
The Reality that Thoughts become Things
That What we Resist Persists

The book is divided into four sections, guiding you on a journey within to release and overcome negative thinking, habits and limiting beliefs that keep you feeling "stuck". These illusions are spellbinding, but this book will help you release these unwanted feelings of low self-esteem, lack and judgment, as well as outdated myths and fears.

A great way to work through these processes is through journaling. Without editing yourself, just allow the words to fall onto the paper. I love keeping a journal next to my bed; I have a few. A yellow one for gratitude, a blue one with a dragonfly on the cover for dreams and another for inspired action which is orange at the moment of writing this. Anything I need to purge and release, I do a brain dump, ceremoniously letting it go.

It is my hope that these pages will help you learn to surf the rise and fall of life's waves of adversity and then recognise your precious gifts as you sail confidently towards your purpose, passion and joy. You can navigate the ocean of life in a way that is unique to you and uncover your hidden treasures of inner wealth on your personal pilgrimage of self- discovery. You can awaken the light within and live with ease, grace and authenticity.

It is my intention that in sharing these processes with you that you will uncover your own innate knowing, start to release the ties that bind and move forward easily and effortlessly as you tune into your own unique SoulFULL path.

I have included a section for you with blank pages at the end for your own Personal Thoughts and Insight.

There are BONUS materials available on my website for you to download, including meditations, PDF's, journal prompts and more. I will continue to add to this over time as I am inspired to create more.

https://ionarussell.com/making-waves-bonus-material/

Wave One

Free Your Mind

You are who you choose to Be.

If you think you will succeed, you will succeed. If you think you will fail, you will fail. If you are looking for validation and gratification externally, you will be lost. It is time for you to begin the journey from within and release the thoughts of who you thought you should be. It is time to align your head and heart as one. It is time to free your mind and tune into the big Mind—the collective consciousness.

The Breath

Let us begin with the breath, and begin where you are.

How are you breathing?

Place your hand on your chest, and notice if your breathing is shallow.
Are your shoulders relaxed or tense? Do you catch yourself holding
your breath?

Notice your breathing . . .

And Now Breathe all the way in through your nose and all the way out
through your mouth . . .

      S....L....O....W...L....Y....

          and consciously and deliberately.

                Lengthening the breath as you go . . .

          Filling your lungs and your tummy.

We tend to hold our tummies in, so relax your tummy, relax your
shoulders and relax your jaw. You can just sit with this if you like, and
that's good.

Again, relax your jaw . . .

Even just 3 conscious breaths like this upon waking can centre you.

Even just a minute will be fab!

Try working up to doing this for 10 minutes.

A Peaceful Practise

You can also add a visualisation on the out breath.
Imagine you are blowing a ribbon out from your mouth,
and you want to keep it afloat in front of you.
(This is one I picked up in yoga.)

Now, let's add in the **HA Breath:**

>This is my favourite go-to breath.
>This is conscious and deliberate breathing.

>>INHALE through your nose . . .

>>EXHALE through your mouth . . .

INHALE Slowly and Deeply, filling your stomach. Allow your stomach to relax and fill your torso and lungs, keeping your shoulders relaxed and your jaw relaxed.

EXHALE . . . making the "HA" sound on the exhale.

>HA as in Alo-HA and HA-waii. It's like a big purposeful sigh.

Rest your hand on your chest, and feel the difference in your exhale as you make this sound, fully and completely emptying your lungs.

To me, this breath feels like a Full Mind, Body and Soul reset.

Do this 3 times or more.

"This breathing is intended to enjoin the presence of the verb of God to heal through emotional evolution."

Harry Uhane Jim

Breathe and Relax
... let your thoughts be and just float off.

We all have so many thoughts going on all at once . . . all the time. And we think we can't have thoughts if we want to meditate. Well, I'm not that enlightened. So what I want you to do is not hold onto the thoughts as they pop in during your meditation.

There are a couple of ways to do this.
Sitting up nice and tall or lying flat with your eyes closed, whenever a thought pops in, just let it be and then let it float off. One thing we know for sure is that a new thought will be along shortly.

Don't fight it; don't be frustrated that it's there. Don't tell yourself not to have a thought (it's like telling yourself to not think about pink elephants), and don't interact with the thought. What do I mean by not interacting with it? Let's say you think, "I forgot to buy milk." That might be true, but then, you may start thinking, "Who forgets to buy milk? Why didn't I just remember I need to buy milk? I'll get it on the way home . . ." That's interacting with the thought rather than just letting "I forgot to buy milk" go.

Meditating for five to ten minutes a day will help calm and relax you. I suggest either breathing normally, or you could breathe in through your nose and out through your mouth in a nice, smooth, natural rhythm.

You might also choose to focus on your breath.

Breathe from your HEART.

Quiet your mind, and in the silence, you will hear your Soul speaking to you.

Consciously breathe in through your nose and out through your mouth with AWARENESS on your HEART.

You will drop down from your head into your HEART.
This is where the magic happens.

You can place your hand on your heart if it helps you.
Do this for three breaths for five minutes or longer.
Do what feels good for you.

Feel like your breath is literally coming in and out of your Heart
Expanded awareness will align your Mind, Body, and Spirit.

"You cannot find your soul with your mind, You must use your heart. You must know what you are feeling. If you don't know what you are feeling, you will create unconsciously. If you are unconscious of an aspect of yourself; if it operates outside your field of awareness, that aspect has power over you."

Gary Zukav

"To find the balance you want, this is what you must become. You must keep your feet grounded so firmly on the earth that it's like you have four legs instead of two. That way, you can stay in the world. But you must stop looking at the world through your head. You must look through your heart, instead. That way, you will know God."

Elizabeth Gilbert

Peace begins with me . . .

Peace

Begins

With

Me

. . . and repeat . . .

This is my favourite mantra for bringing Inner Peace in any given moment.

These words help when feeling overwhelmed, nervous, anxious, or frustrated. Saying these words and breathing deeply and consciously will bring you back to yourself in the present moment.

A Peaceful Practise

You can add in mudras or hand movements.

Tap each finger to your thumb, starting with your
first finger out to your pinky finger, as you say each word.

1st finger = Peace

2nd finger = Begins

3rd finger = With

Pinky finger = Me!

and REPEAT

This redirects your mind, reduces stress
and brings you back to the present moment.

Self-Talk

What are you saying to yourself?

We have an average of 40,000 thoughts a day. Of these, more than 95% of them are a repeat of the thoughts from the day before. What are you repeating to yourself?

Choose your Thoughts and Words wisely.
Would you talk to your best friend the way you talk to yourself?

The quality of your day is dependent on your thoughts.

The cells in your body react to all of your thoughts, and disempowering thoughts weaken your immune system.

So are your thoughts EMPOWERING or DISEMPOWERING?
You really are just a thought away from the day you want.

I struggled for years with feelings of not being enough—not thin enough, pretty enough, successful enough, not enough compared to everyone else. I dealt with self-loathing, eating disorders and clinical depression. So I know it can be a struggle.

START where you are.
Start with you.
Start with learning to **LOVE** and accept yourself
Just as **YOU** are!

"Feelings come and go
like clouds in a windy sky.
Conscious breathing
is my anchor."

Thich Nhat Hanh

Feelings and Thoughts come and go.

You can guarantee another thought will be along shortly.

Breathe deeply, and let your thoughts be as they are. But don't get attached to them.

Observe them.

Let them float and pass by like clouds.

Notice: Are they EMPOWERING or Disempowering?

Notice what you notice
. . . and Breathe . . .
Then, you get to choose how you engage or react or not, as the case might be.

A Peaceful Practise

Imagine you have a chalkboard in front of you.
When a thought appears, imagine wiping it
away with an eraser.

*"Jonathan Seagull discovered that boredom and fear
and anger are the reasons that a gull's life is so short,
and with these gone from his thought, he lived a
long fine life indeed."*

Richard Bach

What are your thoughts creating in your life?
Freedom to Soar or Fall?

What is holding you back from creating a full and glorious life?
Release yourself from disempowering thoughts that keep you stuck.

What is Freedom to you?
When do you feel Free?
When do you Feel most like yourself?
Free to be YOU!

For me, it's teenage laughter and rites of passage,
Ceilidh dancing,
Jumping boomerang,
North Shore Beaches and
Late night freedom on Iona Island.

"To know yourself as the Being underneath the thinker, the stillness underneath the mental noise, the love and joy underneath the pain, is freedom, salvation, enlightenment."

Eckhart Tolle

Intention is Everything

Nothing has ever been accomplished without it.

What is your intention?

How do you want to BE, Feel?

Decide!

Now . . .

Get up . . .

Take Action!

Imperfect Action!

Intention-Setting, Creating, Manifesting, Being in Flow doesn't mean sitting around waiting for the Magic to come to you. TAKE ACTION, and lean into Trusting the Process.

Daily Intentions

How do you want your day to BE?

Set your intention at the beginning of the day.
Focus on how YOU WANT to BE and FEEL!

You get to choose how you want to show up in your day.
Do you want to be Calm, Inspired, Curious, Fun, Carefree . . .?

How you start your day is so important. We've all had those wonderful days when everything just seems to flow and go our way. We get green lights the whole way to our meeting, the sun is shining on the day we have a picnic in the park with family, all our plans are on point and we are smiling. We view the day as easy, and we feel Fabulous.

Then, on the flip side, we've all had those days when we get out of bed on the wrong side, we stub our toe and cuss as we stumble across the room, we have no milk for our coffee and then, we hit every red light on the way to work. We view the day as being sucky, and it is.

But you can choose how you want your day to FEEL—easy and fabulous or sucky and frazzled. Start your day setting Your intention as to how you want to FEEL. I'm not saying that sucky things won't happen some days, but you won't get so overwhelmed by them.

You can choose how you want to BE.

A Peaceful Practise

Start by coming to the present moment.

Pause

Breathe . . .

Inhale, Exhale,

Inhale, Exhale.

Breathe with your hand on your HEART.

Think about how you want to FEEL.

You choose the feeling.

Focus on it and what it means to you.

What that FEELS like.

Imagine this feeling growing.

FEEL the feeling radiating from your HEART centre and
filling every fibre of your body.

FEEL the feeling and how it will be for you in the NOW.

Then, carry the feeling forward with YOU for the whole day.

At any point in the day, if you feel yourself going off course,
you can come back to this feeling easily, having already set the intention.

Put your hand on your heart and breathe. Feel the feeling again.

It just takes a moment to do this.

"We can only BE what we give ourselves the Power to BE!"

Cheroke Saying

What do you give yourself the Power to BE?
What is YOUR Intention?
What is your Soul Goal?

We're not talking about regular Goals here—not the "I want to BE successful" or "I want to have money" goals.

We are looking for your intention behind your Goal.
What's your why?
That's your Goal with SOUL!
Why do you want to be successful?
Why do you want to have money?

Whatever your automatic response is, that's not the answer. Go deeper! It's in the deeper WHY!

How do you want to Feel?
Why?

How do you want to Be?
Why?

How do you want to BE in the world, in your relationships, in your work, in your family?

Why? Go Deeper . . .

What do you want to DO with your life that will facilitate how you want to FEEL and BE?

What do you want to HAVE?

Focus on your intentions—the Goals with Soul. Then, allow and TRUST that the How will follow.

"Within us is a tumultuous ocean of feeling. When we are caught in these currents of mental unrest, all we see is conflict. Through feeling those feelings and allowing them to unwind we return to calmness."

Alain & Jody Herriott

"Everything is energy, Match the frequency of the reality you want, and you cannot help but get that reality."

Darryl Anka

As my dear friend Ali said, "like attracts like", so be the energetic match, the frequency of the reality you want to be in. How will you BE, FEEL, DO and HAVE in this reality you seek? BE that.

You can be all you Dream of, and it starts with giving yourself permission. You are an energy magnet. Everything is Energy!

What are you attracting and creating in your life?

A Peaceful Practise

If you're struggling with this, take a look at what
you're focusing on and how you're showing up.
Are you unintentionally focusing on what you don't want,
such as a lack of abundance and how much it's affecting you,
rather than focusing on what you do want?
Start small!
Embody how it will feel to be immersed in the reality you want —
the life you desire.
Imagine it and visualise it and FEEL it as IF it is your reality right now.

"It's a funny thing about life, once you begin to take note of the things you are grateful for, you begin to lose sight of the things that you lack."

Germany Kent

Practise Daily Gratitude

On waking, gratitude can be as simple as appreciating your soft sheets, your cup of coffee, the fresh air whilst you walk your dog, the JOY you see in your dog running around or the two minutes of peace you suddenly and unexpectedly get even if it's in the car at a red light. Beginning and ending each day with GRATITUDE and APPRECIATION really does change YOUR outlook and wellbeing on a deep Heart and Soul level.

Practise daily gratitude, and watch the MAGIC unfold and increase exponentially.

The secret to gratitude is to FEEL it, truly FEEL gratitude rather than just a statement of thanks. Make it a *feeling* of gratitude.

A Peaceful Practise

Start every day with Gratitude.

Even do this before getting up.

Gratitude is looking for what you LOVE and APPRECIATE.

It's Looking for what you already HAVE.

KEEP it SIMPLE

Try these three for starters:

1) Something you appreciate about yourself.

2) Right NOW, what do you notice—see, hear, feel or sense that you are Grateful for?

3) Something you appreciate about someone else.

A Peaceful Practise

Do this daily.

It's the Attitude of Gratitude.

"Thank you' is the best prayer that anyone could say. I say that one a lot. Thank you expresses extreme gratitude, humility, understanding."

Alice Walker

"In the realm of thought, there are two main categories: thoughts of love and thoughts of fear. Every single moment, we choose between the two. If I think with love, then I am more likely to behave lovingly and to attract love from others. If my heart is closed, I am more likely to act out of fear. Fear-based behavior tends not to look like fear but like anger or jealousy; it elicits reactions from others that reflect my fear and not my love."

Marianne Williamson

How are you showing up in your life?

What is being mirrored back to you?
We get to choose how we show up, and we get to choose how
we co-create our reality.

A Peaceful Practise

Where are you feeling in pain, with fear-based emotions . . .
such as hurt, anger, jealousy or anxiety?
Be honest.
Shine a light on these feelings, with LOVE.
Visualise literally shining a light of LOVE onto yourself,
your pain and your situation.
Feel this LOVE filling your soul.
Trust the process.

What's To-Do?

Do you have a to-do list a mile long?
How do you feel when you can't accomplish everything on your list?
Not great, right?
You might beat yourself up and feel disheartened, overwhelmed and/or disappointed.

We don't want to invite these feelings into our lives!
So ditch the long list. Scrap it; don't do it. Throw it in the bin!

Now, I'm not saying you shouldn't plan and make a TO-DO list—just that there's no point in creating more stress in your life where you don't need it.

It's that simple.
Yes, I know you have some big projects on the go, but as they say, Rome wasn't built in a day. Break your big jobs down into manageable bits.

Here's an extreme example to make my point: If you're building a house, putting "build house" on your list isn't going to help you achieve anything other than feeling overwhelmed. It's too big and too general. It's going to be a long list that you will never achieve today. Not useful!

So what **three** things can you complete today?

A Peaceful Practise

What three things can you realistically complete today?

If you can't do it today, don't put it on the list.

Break it down into bite-sized chunks.

"Happiness cannot be traveled to, owned, earned, worn or consumed. Happiness is the spiritual experience of living every minute with love, grace, and gratitude."

Denis Waitley

What do you need to do to create the life you want?

Think about where you want to be in 12 months. What are the steps to get there? Are you willing to do them?
If not, let this go.
Yes, it's that simple.

For example, I've never had a six-pack, and I never will. It isn't because I can't; it's because I'm not willing to put in the time and effort to get there. So that's one less thing for me to worry about. No point beating myself up about not having a six-pack. I am not staying stuck in a cycle of "woe is me" about my lack of a six-pack. It's my choice to not do this, so now, I can move on and focus on what I am willing to do.

This is my choice!

A Peaceful Practise

What do YOU choose to change or let go of?

BE honest with yourself.

"At any moment you truly have a choice that will either lead you closer to Your Spirit, Your innate Wisdom, Your Intuition. . . or Further away from it."

Thich Nhat Hanh

How amazing and Magnificent is that?
To know that you can change the direction of your
journey at any moment.
What do you choose to do today?

You have the Choice.
You can take the Chance
and Change anything in your life.

Seriously!
If you want your life to change, you have to take action,
and you must take a chance on yourself.
This is your choice!

What do you choose?
It's up to you; it really is.
You get to choose even when it feels like you're stuck.

Thinking about being stuck keeps you there. Stuck in your thinking, stuck in repeating the cycle you're in . . . Stuck still. Still struggling, still broke, still alone, still uninspired, still unhappy . . . still stuck!

Breaking free from thoughts that are keeping you stuck is easier than you think.

The choice is yours. What do you choose?

"Do not become a stranger to yourself by blending."

Dodinsky

Jump out of the box!

Do you sometimes think there must be more than "this"?
What makes you different?
Are you trying to fit in, blend in and do everything that you think you should?
Trying to fit into a box?

The world needs your uniqueness!
Be You.
Embrace your Quirks—
Your Wild Heart.

Run Barefoot along the shore.
Let your Inner Spark Shine Bright.
Radiate!
Light the way!
Burst Free!
Be You.

A Peaceful Practise

What are your unique qualities?

What makes you YOU?

SELF-LOVE

To love yourself is to accept yourself just as you are—
Not when you lose the weight,
Not when you have a perfect relationship, get the job, become a better parent, have the house, have more confidence or have less anxiety.
Accept yourself just as you are right **NOW**, and watch the magic happen!

Too many people are trying to fit into the box

You darling get to break out of the box and break FREE

A Peaceful Practise

If you had to redesign your personality,
what three qualities would you KEEP?
Write them down.

*"It's not who you are
that holds you back;
it's who you THINK you are not
that holds you back!"*

Denis Waitley

You are Everything!

Everything you need—your courage, strength, compassion, love—is already within you.
Everything you seek is within you already. Everything you need is right there inside you.
You were born amazing, confident and perfect, but along the way, you've forgotten that.

Sometimes, we forget it was ever there. Sometimes, we doubt ourselves. We look for "it" outside of us. We look for validation and acceptance externally.

Stop!
Pause!
You can reset yourself, just like a factory restore of your own internal self—back to You!
You are Amazing!

You were born knowing you are Magnificent, Confident, Courageous, Compassionate, Loved, Perfect and knowing that the Possibilities for you are Limitless.
This knowing is still there within you!
Do you remember?
Do You remember how Amazing You Are?
You are Magnificent,
You are Confident,

You are Courageous,

You are Compassionate,

You are Loved,

You are Perfect . . .

and the Possibilities are Limitless

A Peaceful Practise

Set a timer for two minutes,

and without overthinking it,

make a list of all your accomplishments.

Get into your own damn lifeboat!

Stop worrying about what everyone else is doing!
Come up with affirmation statements for yourself. Make them personal,
make them powerful and make them authentic to YOU.
None of this generic shizzle!
Your personal affirmations are your own mantra.

I'm not a fan of "fake it till you make it."
If you can say it and FEEL it and BELIEVE it, then go for it!

If you're not feeling it, you'll just have that negative gremlin bashing you
from the sidelines and trying to throw you overboard without a life vest.

Step up the energy vibe, and like yourself more than you did yesterday,
even if it's just baby steps.

Please see energy diagram
https://ionarussell.com/making-waves-bonus-material/

A Peaceful Practise

Create Your Affirmation Mantras,

and say your mantras to yourself daily.

Examples:

I like myself.

I like myself more than yesterday.

I am okay.

I am Important.

I am Awesome.

I'm excited about the future.

I am making positive changes every day.

I am **Unique.**

I Am

I am!!!

The words that follow "I AM" are Powerful.

What are you telling yourself every day, over and over and over again?

Research shows that 95% of our daily thoughts are a repeat of the day before! That's freaking epic. Now, add to this that our unconscious mind believes what we tell it. This is why Olympic athletes use visualisation in their training.

So what are you repeatedly telling yourself daily? **Think about this!**

Choose your words wisely.

I am Wonderful.

I am Beautifully unique.

I am Happy.

I am an Amazing mother.

I am a Loving father.

I am Calm.

I am Abundant.

I am Successful.

I am Strong.

I am Loved.

I am Loving.

How we choose to talk to ourselves is so Powerful!
You can choose to Empower or Disempower yourself.
Choose your words wisely.

A Peaceful Practise

YOU get to choose how YOU
show up each and every day!
Who do you choose to BE?
I AM........
You have the Power!

I AM......

I am a woman, a mother, a friend, a lover, a goddess.

You have called me stupid, weirdo, strange.
You have called me difficult, too bossy, too commanding, too much, too loud.

I am none of those things.
I am adventurous,
I am unique,
I am unexpected,
I am inquisitive,
I am a leader,
I am creative,
I am outspoken.

I am so much more than enough.
I am all I need me to be, and I am growing, evolving into so much more than this.
I am a strong spiritual woman having a human experience.
I am vulnerable, feminine, compassionate.

You said I couldn't save everyone.
I say I can.
I can do my part,
One person at a time,

One gesture at a time,
One thought at a time,
One intention at a time,
One kindness at a time.
One ripple goes on and on and on and on, and so it goes.

I am connected to everything.
I am huge.
I am all of these things.
I am connected to the infinite loving universe.

I wrote this when I was processing some blocked energy from a
relationship that went low vibe, but these things get said about so many
of US!

The magic happens outside the box.
You are the Magic!
You are Magnificent!

A Peaceful Practise

Journal Prompt:
I am . . .

"Sometimes your joy is the source of your smile,
and sometimes your smile is the source of your joy."

Thich Nhat Hanh

What brings you Joy?

For me, it's the simple things—a walk in the sunshine, hearing my son laugh, breathing deeply by the ocean, a book that I can't put down, playing board games with my son . . .

What brings you joy?
Follow your Joy!

If what you're doing doesn't light you up,
If it doesn't light your Soul on Fire.
STOP doing it.

Do what lights you up!
Do what inspires you.
Try something you've always wondered about doing.
Follow your curiosity—you just might be surprised at where it leads.
Find your limits, and push through them to Joy!

A Peaceful Practise

Divide a sheet of paper in half.
On one side, make a list of all the
things you enjoy doing.
On the other side, make a list of all
the things you are curious about trying.
Look at the lists.
Keep adding to them.
Go out and do something that you enjoy.

*"Learn to master your thoughts and watch closely
what you deposit into your spirit. Speak over your life.
Living in peace has transformative power."*

Germany Kent

Lookout Binoculars

Look out for your thoughts as they appear on the horizon.

Are they empowering or disempowering?

Observe your thoughts, and notice what you notice about them. Be
gentle with yourself. If you notice disempowering thoughts, that's okay.
The good news is that you've spotted them. Now, you're aware of them.
That's a start. Just notice your thoughts, and don't become attached
to them. Allow them to be and float past like a cork bobbing by on the
ocean or a cloud passing across the sky.

You don't need to struggle with your thoughts. It isn't a battle of wills.

Once we start to notice our thoughts for the fleeting moments they
are, we don't need to get caught up with them.

A Peaceful Practise

Let go of your thoughts.
By letting them go, I don't mean to save them for later!
I literally mean to let them go.
Don't dwell on them.
They are gone, and so it is!

Happiness is an inside job!

"Many people think excitement is happiness. . . .
But when you are excited you are not peaceful.
True happiness is based on peace."

Thich Nhat Hanh

It took me years to figure this out!

I was always looking for happiness as a "high" to be maintained—as excitement and stimulation. Being busy, looking for the next thing to "do", the next party, the next activity, hustle and bustle—anything to keep my energy high.

But then, I'd notice how low I felt by comparison in the silence and calm afterwards. Sometimes, I was okay being peaceful, but only temporarily. It was just a stop gap until the next exciting thing. Then, at my lowest low, I started seeking out peaceful practises, as I realised what I was doing wasn't working. And meditation was the start of my new journey. It was a path that I resisted for years and turned my back on, having been raised by Buddhist parents.

Meditation doesn't have to be sitting cross-legged for hours. It's any Practise that you are fully present for, including walking, dancing, yoga, painting, drawing, drinking coffee, looking at your view—anything where you are fully in the moment. That's meditation!

On this journey, I have found that inner peace is where the magic is. That's where happiness is.

She's been there all along. I was just too noisy to notice.

Happiness is an inside job!

"May Your Joys Be As Deep As the Ocean."

Irish Blessing

Wave Two

Release Your Shadow

What is holding you back, keeping you small,

keeping you stuck?

It's time to release yourself from the shadows. To step out

from behind the mask that you have been hiding behind.

It's time to release the ties that bind and remember who

you were born to be. Look for what and who is triggering

you. Therein lies the truth of what you need to release.

Who do you need to forgive?

"If you don't make peace with your past, it will keep showing up in your present."

Wayne Dyer

All journeys start with forgiving yourself and others.
As Harry Uhane Jim (*Wise Secrets of Aloha*) says, you have two choices:
You can forgive now or forgive later.
Who do you need to forgive?

Let go of the ties that bind you to the past in this lifetime.
Your Parents.
Your Grandparents.
Your Ancestors.

We learn conscious and unconscious patterns from our family environment and culture. We can take on these ways of BEing without even knowing or wanting to do so. Our parents learnt from their parents and culture, and so it goes back to the beginning of time. What patterns are you repeating?

A Peaceful Practise

Light a candle for your elders and meditate.

Thank your ancestors.

Journal.

(You can seek help with ancestral clearing, if you need it.)

Ho'oponopono - Hawaiian Healing Prayer

I'm Sorry
Please Forgive me
Thank you
I love you

A Peaceful Practise

What are you sorry to your self for?

What can you ask forgiveness for . . . from yourself?

BE thankful to yourself.

Love yourself.

To my mother. I love you.
And to my mother's mother. Her mother.
And to all mothers from now until the beginning of time.
I love you.

To my father. To my dad. To his dad.
And to all dads from now until the beginning of time.
I love you.

I am the sum total of all my ancestors.
To all my descendants in the feminine. I love you.
To all my descendants in the male. I love you.

I am the sum total of the potential of all my descendants.
I hold this space in the name of my mother and all mothers.
I hold the spark of life from my father and all fathers
to the beginning of time.

I commit to be aware that I am the sum total of all
my ancestors and all my descendants.
I am never alone.

Harry Uhane Jim

This is my favourite version of the Ho'oponopono prayer, from *Wise Secrets of Aloha: Talk Story with Hawaiian Healer, Harry Uhane Jim.* I had the honour of sitting in circle with him at his healing hut on the Big Island of Hawaii along with my fellow Aloha KCR family. He is a special Soul.

For me this is about releasing all our ancestral ties within our family, as well as others we encounter who bring down our vibe, trigger us, and teach us. We are all family.

A Peaceful Practise

Meditate on this prayer.

This prayer is quoted from the series at https://vimeo.com/search/ondemand?q=wise+secrets+of+aloha, May 2016 -September 2016.

Ebb and Flow

Just as the tide ebbs and flows,

So does Life.

Nothing is permanent.

Everything is Energy.

Waves

Emotion

Situations and Circumstances

Trust—

This, too, shall pass.

"Everything is energy. Your thought begins it, your emotion amplifies it and your action increases the momentum."

Unknown

Everything is Energy.

Are you holding on to emotions that are holding you back?
Release and let go of negativity, anger, guilt and resentment so that you are clear and open-hearted.

Let it go so that you can grow.
Start by forgiving yourself!

Release and let go of your past.

Learn to break free from what's holding you back, and get on with creating the life you want. You are just one thought away from an amazing day. It's time to let go and forgive.

A Peaceful Practise

At night before you go to bed, FORGIVE
everything, and
sleep with a clean pure HEART.
It might take practise,
but letting go is POWERFUL.

"There are two basic motivating forces: fear and love. When we are afraid, we pull back from life. When we are in love, we open to all that life has to offer with passion, excitement, and acceptance. We need to learn to love ourselves first, in all our glory and our imperfections. If we cannot love ourselves, we cannot fully open to our ability to love others or our potential to create. Evolution and all hopes for a better world rest in the fearlessness and open-hearted vision of people who embrace life."

John Lennon

You are either living in
Love or Fear.

Do you focus on your fears or on love? Wherever you focus is where your energy will go and also exactly what you will attract.

What do you want to attract into your life—more fear or more love?

If you're holding onto guilt, shame, anger or sadness, you are holding onto fear and limiting your ability to create the life you want.

These negative emotions are baggage you carry with you. They are heavy, and they rob you of energy. Lack of forgiveness is much like a roadblock on the path to peace of mind and the life you want. They are the result of judging yourself or others. By holding onto the past, you hold onto fear.

So shift your attention, and forgive any transgressions from yourself or others. When you learn to let go of judgement, you can forgive and move forward, replacing the negativity with love rather than fear. Only then can you let go of the victim mentality and be empowered with love.

It's time to let it go.

"Placing the blame or judgment on someone else leaves you powerless to change your experience; taking responsibility for your beliefs and judgments gives you the power to change them."

Byron Katie

A Peaceful Practise

Do you need to forgive someone?

Contemplate this.

Can you forgive them?

Do you need to forgive yourself?

Can you forgive yourself?

This isn't about blame.

It's about acceptance and choosing LOVE!

Are you okay?

What if the only thing wrong with you is that you THINK there's something wrong with you?

Read that again!

What do you think about yourself?
Do you think you are Amazing?
Do you think you are Magnificent?
Do you think you are Beautiful?
Do you think you are Brilliant, Inspiring,
Kind, Loved, Loving, Fabulous . . .?

Or do you think you aren't clever enough, thin enough, pretty enough, too fat, too thin, not fast enough, successful enough? Do you think you aren't enough?

You are Wonderful as you are!
So what do you REALLY think of yourself?

A Peaceful Practise

Write yourself a LOVE Letter

What do you appreciate about yourself?

What are your natural gifts?

*"Success is liking yourself and liking
what you do and how you do it."*

Maya Angelou

It took a long time for me to realise that the missing link was liking myself first before I could be happy with anything or anyone else. From the outside, I appeared happy and confident. But I wasn't on the inside. It took lots of trial and error to figure it out.

And the thing that saved me was breathing, BEing present and BEing mindful.

It's that simple!

That's where my recovery from self-sabotage, overwhelm and unhappiness began. Are you breathing deeply and consciously?

A Peaceful Practise

Don't forget to make time to meditate daily!
Meditation doesn't need to be you sitting in a cave or on top of a hill.
Do something that fits into your day.
When are you most mindful and present?

It can be when you are walking, drawing, painting, singing.
Whatever it is, do MORE of that!
BE Fully Present!

"Wherever you go, go with all your heart."
Confucius

To transform yourself, change your thinking!
ReBoot YOU back to your innate default settings of Magnificence!
You ARE Born Amazing!

You are Made in the Spiritual image and Likeness of the Divine,
Universal Love.

It is in the disconnect that we look outside ourselves for gratification,
approval and belonging. It is our environment and our experiences that
create and reinforce our thinking, beliefs, patterns and behaviours—both
empowering and disempowering—that we adopt as real, as our own.

A Peaceful Practise

What limiting beliefs are you willing to let go of today?

Whose beliefs are they?

Journal about them!

Release the Suck

Release what's sucking the life out of your joy. What drains your energy and distracts you from being inspired and SoulFUL?

Maybe you're scrolling on Facebook or Instagram, comparing yourself to others. Maybe you're caught in a Netflix vortex. Maybe you're hanging around with folks that keep you small and keep you down with their negative chatter. Maybe you're drowning in "shoulds". (Let's call these the dreaded Should Gremlins.) Maybe you're rushing around, putting everyone else first and leaving no time for yourself.

Whatever is sucking your life force, STOP IT!

STOP & RELEASE THE SUCK!

What are you going to release?
What's sucking the light from your BEing?

What are you going to STOP doing today?
Do it Now!

And Now, you've made room for your SOUL to be Filled
                            with something that LIGHTS You up!

A Peaceful Practise

Stop doing something that is sucking your life force.

What are you going to stop doing?

Clutter in your environment stops the energy of energy.

Declutter.

Make room for new energy into your life.

Return to Love and
Choose Your Tribe

"Our deepest fear is not that we are inadequate. Our deepest fear is that we are powerful beyond measure. It is our light, not our darkness that most frightens us. We ask ourselves, 'Who am I to be brilliant, gorgeous, talented, fabulous?' Actually, who are you not to be? You are a child of God. Your playing small does not serve the world. There is nothing enlightened about shrinking so that other people won't feel insecure around you. We are all meant to shine, as children do. We were born to make manifest the glory of God that is within us. It's not just in some of us; it's in everyone. And as we let our own light shine, we unconsciously give other people permission to do the same. As we are liberated from our own fear, our presence automatically liberates others."

— Marianne Williamson

Read that again!

OMGosh, this is liberating and empowering!
You are Magic, and You are meant to Shine.
So Shine, baby, Shine.

Williamson's book *Return to Love* opened my heart and eyes to all the infinite possibilities I have and helped me embrace who I am. All of me! I started to discover my own inner happiness, which had been there all along. But I'd been hiding it behind all the things I thought I *should* do, inadvertently playing the victim of my own story.
Little did I know that this was also the path towards being single again.

Where are you hiding out?
What are you avoiding?
What secrets do you keep?
What are you afraid of?
Who are you?

Are you amongst the people who "get" you?
Do they inspire you?
Do they make you Laugh?
Do you feel safe and supported with them?
Are you creating amazing projects together?

You get to choose your tribe!

A Peaceful Practise

Who are you surrounding yourself with?
If you are still looking for your tribe,
look at what interests you and what you are drawn to.
Go to where these interests and activities are happening.
You can find your tribe there!

"When you come out of the storm

you won't be the same

person who walked in.

That's what this storm's all about."

Haruki Murakami

"True power is living the realization that you are your own healer, hero, and leader."

Yung Pueblo

What beliefs are you holding onto that are holding you back?

What beliefs are keeping you in dis-ease and lack?

Whose beliefs are they?

What is your attitude about relationships?

Money?

What do you believe about your health?

Fitness?

Do you think you will be successful, or do you have thoughts of not being enough?

Do you think, "Who am I to do that?" or "I can't!" or "No one from my family has ever . . .?"

What patterns are you repeating in your life that your parents and grandparents repeated?

A Peaceful Practise

Make a list of what is holding you back.

Include your beliefs about your limits.

Sit with these "thoughts" for a few moments.

Are they yours?

Are they true?

Are they *really* true?

"We can't be afraid of change. You may feel very secure in the pond that you are in, but if you never venture out of it, you will never know that there is such a thing as an ocean, a sea. Holding onto something that is good for you now, may be the very reason why you don't have something better."

C. JoyBell C.

Do you want something more?
Do you doubt you can have something more?

Doubt is like a toxin that seeps into your system.

Let go of the outcome.
Sometimes, what happens is way better than you could have ever dreamt possible.

Be open to the unknown, the unexpected.
That's where the MAGIC is—in the unknown.

A Peaceful Practise

Where are you holding yourself back?
Why?
What is there to be gained in staying still or moving forward?
Our mind believes that staying in our comfort zone is keeping us
safe.
Are you stuck in your comfort zone?
Do you want to break free?
Are you willing to be uncomfortable?

We gain power over a belief when we remember to question it.
What patterns and behaviours are you unconsciously repeating that are
not in your best interest?

Which ones are not in alignment with who you want to Be?
Not What you want to Do?
Not How you want to Feel?

What belief or habit is driving you? Do you feel out of control? These
patterns and behaviours can be uncovered and shifted a lot quicker than
you might think.

What changes Do you want to make?
Are you stuck in overwhelm? Procrastination? Unhealthy lifestyle
choices?
Food?
Are you a worrier?
Are you sad and anxious?
Maybe you're doing great but keep self-sabotaging. Yet, you don't
know why. Maybe you appear to be thriving, but inside, you're battling
imposter syndrome.

We can have so many beliefs and patterns that we've picked up from
other people. They are outdated and not truly ours! It's time to question
those beliefs and release them.

You can do this!

You can make the changes you want!

You are enough!

You are magnificent!

You are perfect!

You can be All you want to be and More!

You can be Happy and Fulfilled!!

Pause and ask yourself what do you want to BE, DO, HAVE and FEEL?

A Peaceful Practise

What language are you using about

who and what you want to BE, Do, Have and Feel?

Is it disempowering and constrictive?

I can't do _____.

It's too hard to _____.

I haven't got time to_____.

Is what you are choosing to focus on going to matter to you in two years?

Can you flip it?

I am choosing to _____.

I can_____.

I choose to_____.

I am _____.

I am working towards_____.

Are you focused on your higher purpose and for the higher good of all?

"Life isn't about waiting for

the storm to pass. . . .

It's about learning to dance in the rain."

Vivian Greene (before Yung Pueblo)

"A real sign of progress is when we no longer punish ourselves for our imperfections."

Yung Pueblo

I am flawed, perfectly.

Embrace your flaws. It's so liberating to accept yourself and love yourself as you are.

I've struggled with how I thought I *should* be, and boy, did it get exhausting! And the crazy thing is these were expectations put on by me. These were expectations I took on that others have said. But I chose to take them on.

I have honestly been my worst critic.
"Not _____ enough". Fill in the blank—thin, funny, successful, good, wild, bad, clever—the list can be endless!

You are enough, I am enough, and our flaws are perfect.

I love you the way you are!

A Peaceful Practise

Can you embrace ALL of you?
What would you say to yourself as your best friend?

We are what we BELIEVE we are!

What beliefs are you telling yourself—consciously or unconsciously?
Are your thoughts positive and encouraging?
PAUSE to check out what you are telling yourself.
Remember: Thoughts become Things!
Your thoughts are powerful
You are what you tell yourself!

A Peaceful Practise

Make a list of ten things that you have done

for yourself in the last ten days.

Not for others!

This is about YOU.

Things that you have enjoyed.

Things that have filled and lit you up.

Look at the list:

What do you need to do more?

Wisdom, not Wounds!

Are you repeating patterns that are negative, self-sabotaging and disempowering?

Where did you learn these patterns and behaviours?

We pass on our wounds and patterns to our children if we don't learn from them and release them.

What issues do you need to resolve?

Think about that for a moment.

Do you want to pass on Wounds or Wisdom? The more you work on your personal issues, the more successful you will be in ending the cycles and sharing Wisdom.

Release your wounds, and let that process create Wisdom. This is alchemy.

A Peaceful Practise

Turn something around that you've been through.

Rather than think it happened "to" me,

think it happened "for" me.

What are the lessons you gained from the experience?

Stagnant
Overwhelm
Drowning

Do you appear to have it all,
but you still feel stuck—trapped in a swamp?

It's like you're stuck in a pond with no flow, and you can't figure out how
to get the energy back to flowing with inspiration, momentum and joy.

A Peaceful Practise

Stir up the waters . . . and get Your Energy Moving.

Breathe!

Dance!

Sing!

Go out for a walk!

Run!

Hold your own light!

When in overwhelm, you can choose to be your own light.

No one else can do it.
You are responsible for you.

No one else.
You get to decide how you show up.

No one else.
It all starts and ends with you darling heart.

No one else.
You Be your own Light.

Own it.
Don't wait for someone else to light your way.

You Hold your own light and OWN IT!

Down days suck.
Allow the feelings to BE.
Feel the feels, but don't hold onto them.
Let them flow, and release them.

It sounds easy, but some days aren't so easy.
We all have our gremlins, but we get to choose how we deal with them.

Chatting with a gardener friend, I described holding onto fears,
negativity, sadness and anger as like blocking the water hose.
Nothing can get through.
We can't water our inner garden and flourish with a blocked hose.
Just like the plants in the garden, we will wither, wilt and die inside.

Release the kinks, and let the feelings flow.
LET GO!

Feed Your Soul.
Tend to your needs.
Listen to what you need.
If you're overwhelmed and stressed, depleted, burnt out, tired or
blocked, you know you need to take time out for yourself!
You're probably busy doing for others.
You need to see the good side of yourself.
Look how far you've come.
Look how much you are appreciated.
Give yourself that appreciation!

You know you need to make YOU a priority.
Take small steps toward self-care.
A spa day or a hot bath.
Something that feeds your SOUL.

A Peaceful Practise

Do something just for you.
Unapologetically!

"Don't believe everything you think."

Thubten Chodron

Are you a worrier or a warrior?

Worrying?
Stuck treading water, unable to move forwards or backwards?
You've lost the oars, and there's no one around to help you steer out of the murky waters of self-doubt and self-sabotage?
What is it you think you believe?

You can kick this habit effectively with mindfulness, Peaceful Practises and some reframing. It really is quicker and easier than you might think.

No more worrier pose!
Let's move into Warrior pose!
What can you do today to Move into Warrior?

A Personal Practise

What are you worrying about? Why?

Examine where you start to say "Because . . ."

PAUSE on this: Go deeper than your

initial automatic response.

Is it true what you're worrying about? Yes or No?

Are you sure?

Who are you with this thought?

Who would you be without this thought?

Triggers are our teachers

Do you get triggered by certain people? Of course, you do. We all do.

When someone triggers you, think loving, kind thoughts toward them.
Find something to be grateful for about them. Appreciate them. Think,
"I LOVE YOU." Do your best to FEEL it in your HEART. Open to the
love available to you, and really feel it. Be sure to breathe deeply!
Sit with this, and see what happens.
I've found that miraculously, the other person's demeanour changes,
and their attitude softens. It's subtle but noticeable.

Triggers are our mirrors, showing us what we need to work on.
What do you see in the other person that you need to work on?
Is it forgiveness?
Patience?
Kindness?
Is it a reflection of you?
We are all cut from the same cloth.
What is being brought into your awareness as a result of the trigger?

A Peaceful Practise

Notice your triggers and what they are
teaching you about yourself.
Journal about them!
When being triggered, focus on LOVE.
Feel it in your HEART.
Feel it towards the person triggering you.
Hold that feeling of LOVE
Hold the Space of LOVE.

Holding on

Only hurts me, not him.

Only punishes me, not him.

Only creates undercurrents of gloom in my life, not his!

A Peaceful Practise

Who are you holding onto?

Release them.

Journal about this.

*"We are all like the bright moon,
we still have our darker side."*

Kahlil Gibran

Secrets lie in our shadows.
A Mirror of reflection
Exposing our Shame
Our Guilt
Fear.
Do you deny this?
Do you hide this?

Shine the light and know we are all cut from the same cloth, and healing happens when we accept all of us as one.

What you seek to heal in others is what you need to heal in yourself.

Everyone is your reflection.

Do you see this?

Release the reflection, and embrace all of who you are.

Accept all that they are.

"If you are willing to look at another person's behaviour toward you as a reflection of the state of their relationship with themselves rather than a statement about your value as a person, then you will, over a period of time cease to react at all."

Yogi Bhajan

A Peaceful Practise

Choose Love!

Choose Acceptance!

Choose Unconditional Love!

"Within you, there is a stillness and a sanctuary to which you can retreat at anytime and be yourself."

Hermann Hesse, Siddhartha

Your Ripple Effect

What are the stories you're telling yourself?

Are you playing small to fit in, dimming your light?

Are you putting your needs first or last?

There is a ripple effect in all that you do.

You teach others how to BE with you, how to treat you and what to expect from you by how you show up or hide out.

What are the ripples you are creating?

Positive?

Empowering?

Inspiring?

Happy?

Be YOU, and BE the change you want to see.

It takes courage to be yourself.

You Be You, and I'll Be Me!

A Peaceful Practise

Begin by making a list of what is important
to you in order of priority.
Think about WHY these things matter to you.
Where are YOU on that list?
If you aren't at the top of your priorities, why not?

Make a list of the qualities that are most important
to you in order of priority.
Are you BEing the person who embodies the qualities you listed?
Go and BE the person who embodies them.

*"Let the waters settle and you will see the moon
and the stars mirrored in your own being."*

Rumi

Let the ripples settle, and choose to be calm. Don't contribute pebbles
to any chaos in your life.

And do not allow others to disturb your inner calm with their own
pebbles of chaos.

A Peaceful Practise

You cannot control anyone else.
Focus on you.
Do not take on anyone else's negative energy,
chaos or behaviours.
Instead, take three deep breaths,
and come back to your centre—your HEART.

Say to YOURSELF, "I love you." FEEL it.

Repeat the Ho'oponopono prayer:
I'm Sorry.
Please Forgive me.
Thank you.
I love you.

"I was never addicted to one thing;
I was addicted to filling a void within myself with
other things other than my own love."

Yung Pueblo

How much do you LOVE yourself? From 1-100?
If it isn't 100, why not?

I used to fill the void within with all sorts of destructive behaviours, unhealthy relationships, substances, food, work, being busy (oh, so busy), overworking, running away—ah, the list goes on. Can you relate?

It took me a long time to finally figure out that I had to heal myself, to love myself. And it started with learning to accept and like **ME** as I am. Letting go of the past, letting go of my expectations for the future, and **BE**ing present.

It wasn't easy, and it took a lot of trial and error. But I can honestly say **I LOVE ME**! I really do. I learnt to love myself fully and completely from the inside out.

A Peaceful Practise

Say to yourself:

I am amazing.

I can do anything.

Positivity is a choice.

I celebrate my individuality.

I am prepared to succeed.

Wave Three

Expand your HEART

Listen to your HEART, live from your HEART, create

from your HEART.

LET LOVE FLOW forth from your HEART.

Love is THE HIGHEST vibration.

Breathe from your Heart.

Align Mind, Body and Spirit through your Heart

Choose Love!

"If the ocean can calm herself so can you.

We are all salt water mixed with air."

Nayyirah Waheed

All change starts and ends with you!
BE Calm
within your Soul.

Heart Vibes Meditation
Pause . . .
How do you want to BE?
Connect with the feelings you want to bring into BEing.
Feel into the Feelings.
Feel into the memory—imagined or real.
Breathe from your HEART.
Be Present.
Smile.

. . . and repeat

Feel the feelings grow and glow.
Feel your HEART Expanding.
Feel the Feelings
Radiating out,
Growing Glowing from your HEART,
Expanding out beyond your physical being
Out into the Universe.

Forgotten Dreams

This sounds like the beginning of a 1980s track: If you have a DREAM, no matter how old, it's never too late. What was that Dream you had as a child—the dream you have now? I'm not necessarily saying you can become the prima ballerina you dreamed of being when you were a child, but maybe you can find a way to embrace dance more.

How can you bring more of what you dream of into your life?

What DREAM fills your HEART?
Walk the Appalachian trail?
Climb Machu Picchu?
Run wild at Burning Man?
Canoe down the River Wye?
Write a Book?
Start a Business?
Paint?
Learn to Sing?

Follow your Dreams.
Follow your Ambitions.
Have faith that it will happen, and it will.

What is it that you are drawn to now?

What inspires you?

When are you most in FLOW?

When have you felt MOST like Yourself?

This book is MY Dream.

A Peaceful Practise

Journal about when you were most in Flow,
when you felt most ALIVE
and most like the REAL YOU!

Are you Inspired?
Take Action.

A Dragon Heart

Bravery is the Courage to live as yourself.

Living Your Truth
From Your Heart!

Are you living your truth?
or are you hiding
behind self-imposed walls,
Afraid to be seen for who you are?
Are you out in the world fighting for what you believe?
Are you a Peaceful Warrior with the Heart of a Dragon?

Do you have a message?
A purpose?
Do you recognise it in yourself?

A Peaceful Practice

What are you drawn to that you do without hesitation?

Why?

Does it light your Heart and Soul on Fire?

Does it raise the vibration?

Do you Dream about it?

Do more of that?

"Dreams are illustrations. . . from the book your soul is writing about you."

Marsha Norman

What is YOUR Dream?

What is YOUR SECRET Dream?

Writing this book is the dream I'd forgotten I always had.
I was going through my mum's old paperwork and found a letter hidden away that I'd sent her when I was 21 years young, while traveling and working in Hawaii. It is filled with the innocent optimism of my youthful philosophising about what I was going to do with my life. I had no plans other than I wanted to one day write a book. I found this letter two weeks after I signed my first publishing deal.

What Dreams do you have waiting to manifest?

What Dreams do you have hidden away in a pile of old paperwork?

Dreams do come True, and yours can, too.

I believe in You, and I believe in your Dreams.

A Peaceful Practise

Sit and meditate on your wildest long-ago dream.
Let the memories speak,
and journal about it.

"Trust in dreams,

for in them is the hidden gate to eternity."

Kahlil Gibran

Happy Glow

You GLOW differently when you are HAPPY.
You feel differently,
And You radiate Sunbeams from the inside out.

How do you feel right now?

Are you feeling Happy right now?
If not, start by finding something to feel genuine Gratitude for.
You can start small, and let the feeling Grow and Glow.

I'm not asking you to fake it till you make it. That saying was always crap
for me when I felt like crap. I would just find that the negative self-talk
immediately started putting me down.
You might have met that particular gremlin yourself. She's a bitch!

So start where you are, and let's take it up a small step.
Small steps each day to raise up your vibe authentically.

See Emotional Vibration chart of feelings on bonus page of website
https://ionarussell.com/making-waves-bonus-material/

"I find it extremely liberating to see that I was the cause of all my problems. With this realization, I have also learned that I am my own solution. This is the great big gift of personal accountability. When we stop blaming external forces and own up to our responsibility, we become the ultimate creators of our destiny."

Jenna Galbut

*"The things that make me different are the
things that make me ME."*

Winnie the pooh

What is wonderful about YOU?
What is great about YOU?
What do other people notice about YOU?
What do you notice about yourself?

Work on the qualities YOU have already!
Amplify YOUR Uniqueness.

Rather than trying to fix your beliefs about your limits,
Focus on what you already have—your own Unique Greatness!

A Peaceful Practise

What are your unique qualities?
Journal about them.

Don't be the same—BE BETTER!

How many times has someone said to you, "You've changed; you're not the same"? Have you then tried to justify yourself, to make excuses to convince them you are the same?

Listen! Own it! "Yes, thank you, I HAVE changed! Thank you for noticing I've changed. I HAVE been Doing THE Work!"

Every time we up-level, it's because we are DOing the work.
We are putting in the time.
We are making the changes that we need to grow and evolve.

Graciously accept the compliment, whether they meant it as one or not. What they think of you is not your concern. "Not my monkeys, not my circus!"

Up levelling means putting in the work!
Up-levelling means noticing a strength you
have and amplifying it for your Higher good.
Up-levelling means seeing a weakness or
trigger as an issue you need to address.

Change doesn't happen overnight, but you get
to choose how you show up!

"Wash the dust from your

Soul and Heart

with wisdom's Water."

Rumi

"Just like a sunbeam can't separate itself from the sun, and a wave can't separate itself from the ocean, we can't separate ourselves from one another. We are all part of a vast sea of love, one indivisible Divine mind."

Marianne Williamson

How yummy is this?

We are like SUNBEAMS and WAVES. We are all part of the Great Beautiful Oneness.
We are not alone! We are never alone.

Sometimes, you may feel alone. You may feel that no one sees you, and you are struggling, feeling stuck and like you don't fit in. You may feel afraid to step out of your current circumstances and makes changes in your career, start a business, a relationship, etc. You may feel afraid to come out into the light and shine.

Reach out! Connect with someone you're curious about. Surround yourself with those who inspire you and believe in you. Maybe it starts with a book of inspiration, a podcast, a Meetup group, a class or a chance encounter with a stranger. Reconnect with an old friend. The possibilities are limitless. YOU are limitless.

I see You.

You are Worthy.

Your Light matters.

You are Magnificent.

And I love You.

"You are not separate from the whole. You are one with the sun, the earth, the air. You don't have a life. You are life."

Eckhart Tolle

You are part of something so much bigger. You are one with the entire Universe. Can you see yourself in that light and love yourself?

Can you accept you are as Magnificent as the sun, the moon and the stars? That you are as Magnificent as the air, water, earth and fire?

You are LOVE!
Love yourself as you are.
Self-Love and self-Acceptance as you are.

Are You Compassionate with yourself?
Do you show Kindness towards yourself?
Are you Forgiving and Patient with yourself?

A Peaceful Practise

Look for the beauty around you.
Know that you are one with the beauty you see.
What you perceive is a reflection of YOU.
Can you see the BEauty around you?

Hawaiian Rules

from *Wise Secrets of Aloha* by Harry Uhane Jim

Never judge a day by the weather.
The best things in life aren't things.
Tell the truth—there's less to remember.
Speak softly and wear a loud shirt.
Goals are deceptive. The unaimed arrow never misses.
He who dies with the most toys—still dies.
Age is relative. When you're over the hill, you pick up speed.
There are two ways to be rich—make more or desire less.
Beauty is internal—looks mean nothing.
No Rain, No Rainbows.

I am named after a small Island off the West Coast of Scotland. Island vibes are in my SOUL—be it the west coast of Scotland or the mid-Atlantic.

Being by water feeds my Soul, so I love these Hawaiian Rules. I urge you to consider them as you let go of hiding your shadows and embrace all of who you are. Transform into who you were born to be for the Higher Good. You can do so light-heartedly and with a twinkle in your eye.

There are many who have shared their interpretation of "Kimo's Hawaian Rules"; What follows is my interpretation.

Never judge a day by the weather.

Do you jump to conclusions in the first moments of a feeling?

In those moments when things feel like negative, like it's just going to be one of those days?

Then that's you decided that is how your day is going to go... from bad to worse, like a bad weather forecast you hold no hope out for sunshine and rainbows.

You get to choose how your day will be from moment to moment.

You get to decide what kind of day you are going to have, regardless of how it looks in that moment, with rain clouds looming.

You are the one who gets to decide to shine, from the inside out.

No matter what the weather

You can be your own sunshine

BE your own shining light

BE the shining light for others to see and lead by example.

A Peaceful Practise

Do you jump to conclusions about how
your day is going to be fore it's happened?
Pause…. is this working for you?

The best things in life aren't things.

What do you value most in your life?

What do you "want"?
A new house, a new motorbike, lavish holidays, the latest designer jeans, the newest shiny gadgets?
Why?
What is it you REALLY Want?
Maybe you are seeking a feeling—a way you want to BE, and you're looking for it in all the wrong places, in the external gratification and validation that you *think* comes in this stuff.

Maybe what you seek is the feeling of Happiness and Joy, but it can't be found in things.

Do you think, "I'll be happy when I have this 'stuff'"?
How about you just get happy NOW?
And then, if you get those other "things," you'll be happy *and* have "stuff".

But your HAPPINESS isn't dependent on things. You are responsible for your own happiness. And if you expect others to make you happy, you'll always end up disappointed.

The best things in LIFE are FEELINGS, not things.

A Peaceful Practise

What feelings are you seeking?
Focus, imagine, and visualise what it feels like.
How will you BE with the feeling of
Happiness, Love, Calm, Honesty, Creativity, Kindness,
Forgiveness, Peacefulness?

Tell the truth—there's less to remember.

BE impeccable with your word.

Tell the Truth to Yourself.

Be honest with yourself, and be Kind. Be *very* Kind. Being honest doesn't mean you have to be brutally honest. So often, we lie to ourselves.

We say, "Tomorrow, I will take care of myself. Tomorrow, I will put myself first. Tomorrow, I will start living my dreams. I will start writing the book I've always dreamed of. I will start running to get fitter. I will eat healthier when I have more time. I will travel. I will sleep more. I will phone that friend I keep thinking about. I will open myself up to love. I will ask for help tomorrow. I will start that business venture next year. I will meditate tomorrow. I will . . . I will . . ."

Instead, start today!

Start now, and tell yourself the TRUTH. Own it!

Own your own Truth.

What is Your Truth?

What are you doing for yourself Now—

right now in this present moment?

Whatever you do, do it with LOVE!

Be impeccable with your word.

Speak to yourself and others kindly.

The words you say and think become the foundations of your beliefs and the expression of your character.

A Peaceful Practise

What truth do you need to tell yourself?

Journal about it.

And do it with LOVE

Speak softly and wear a loud shirt.

Speak softly and wear a loud shirt. I'm not suggesting you literally wear a loud shirt, but if you feel inclined, please do so. Wear it if it makes you happy. It's what we DO that matters. Our Actions Speak LOUDER than our Words.

So what are you saying with your words?
What are you saying with your actions?

Do you say that you are kind and peaceful, but your actions show otherwise? How do you treat the waitress? The bank teller? The taxi driver? The mother with a child crying at the airport? What are your thoughts even if you aren't speaking them out loud?

Live with integrity, in all that you DO!
You don't need to shout out about your good deeds, good intentions, or your goodness. It will show in your actions and in the way you are in the world.

A Peaceful Practise

What are your thoughts about other people?
Are they in integrity with what you say?

Goals are deceptive—the unaimed arrow never misses.

This might sound counterintuitive. It doesn't mean to never set goals, however. It simply means to relax and do more of what you enjoy. Follow the Feelings and Intentions, and see where that leads you. The road to Happiness leads to success.

So many people talk about having Goals and aiming for them, but how many of you have had a goal that you didn't reach and then felt like a failure? Then, we are told we just need to try harder, aim better, do more.

We say to ourselves, "I'll be happy when . . ." or "I will know I am a success when . . ." It's always looking toward a future state that sets us up for failure.

Instead, look at your INTENTION behind the goal. What is your WHY? How do you want to FEEL, BE, DO and HAVE in the process? And BE PRESENT!

Also, if you do reach the Goal, it might not bring satisfaction. The Fitbit is a great example of this. Most people start with 10,000 steps, and when they reach this, they increase the number, never feeling satisfied, or they become obsessed with doing more. That was me!

Goals can be limiting, too. Most of us aren't aware of our full potential and may inadvertently limit or stagnate our progress with a mediocre goal compared to what we really can accomplish.

As you can see, I'm not a fan of traditional goal-setting. Instead, I urge you to discover your WHY and how you want to Be, Feel, Do and Have. Make that the intention/strategy.

It's all hidden in plain sight in the WHY!

A Peaceful Practise

Look at your Goals.

Do you know what your deeper Why is?

He who dies with the most toys—still dies.

You can't take it with you, so you might as well take the time you have on this earth and make the BEST of it. How do you choose to make use of your time? Life is about BE-ing rather than having the most toys.

What matters to you?

A Peaceful Practise

What do you spend most of your time focused on?

Age is relative—when you're over the hill, you pick up speed.

What does ageing mean to you?

Appreciate the knowledge that comes with living.
As we age, we may lose some of our abilities, but we gain so much!

Being young is fun and wild. You run around exploring, learning and experiencing.
But High Energy can also be chaotic.
Then, you may slow down with age, but you also gain Wisdom.
We continue to grow, and our personal development and spiritual awareness might actually pick up speed.

We get to choose how we age.
Grow and continue to learn, and you age gracefully.

A Peaceful Practise

What does ageing mean to you?
What does Wisdom does to you?
Journal on this.

There are two ways to be rich—make more or desire less.

An abundance of Riches is more than just finances or material things. It's about Health, Happiness and Love, too.

For material things, you know how to get more, but what if you desire less? Feel Gratitude for what you have, and you will be Happier. Be present in this moment and appreciate everything.

Gratitude + Happiness = Success

Happiness brings success, not the other way round.

A Peaceful Practise

You can create a life with more Abundance, Health, Happiness and Love.
Choose what you focus on.
Choose the way you want to FEEL, BE, DO, HAVE.
Choose your PURPOSE.
What is the outcome you want?
Choose and go for it!

Beauty is Internal—looks mean nothing.

Think of the people in your life who have touched you and who have had a positive impact on your life—big or small. Do you consider their looks? What is it you remember about them right now—their Hearts, their compassion, their actions, how they made you feel?

Now, let's flip this around. How do you think people remember you?

You become memorable to other people by the way you made them feel, by how you behave, how you inspired and motivated them or how you helped them.

Beauty that radiates from the inside out is memorable! It shines brightly like sunbeams from your Heart and Soul to theirs.

A Peaceful Practise

How do you think people remember you?

What do you think people think you care about
based on how you behave?
What would people be surprised to know
you actually care about?
Journal on this.

No Rain—No Rainbows.

What does this mean to you? For me, it's about appreciating the contrasts of the journey we are on. Of knowing that there is beauty and lessons to be learnt in everything we go through.

We may want the sun shining forever in our lives and for life to only be positive and easy. But I've lived in places where the sunshine gets brutal, and your skin dries out and starts to burn. Rain is a welcome relief and brings the necessary balance.

We need this contrast and balance. We see light because of the contrast with the dark. We need to experience all kinds of weather.

Think about the weather you enjoy. There will be someone somewhere who prefers the opposite because of their environment. I'm in Scotland now and LOVE hot sunny days. When I lived in Texas, I loved cloudy and rainy days. (This is about contrast, of course, not about the locations themselves.)

How many of you get EXCITED when you see a rainbow? I do! This year seems to have been a magical year for rainbows. They always stop me in my tracks.

Happiness and Joy are not destinations we reach if we ignore the storms, the negativity, the dark and the shadows. Happiness is about weathering the storm, going through adversity, learning from it and creating opportunities and infinite possibilities from it.

Sunshine and rain are necessary for you to have RAINBOWS in your life.

A Peaceful Practise

What storms have you come through?
You are here and you got through the storm.

What are the rainbows that have resulted from the storm?
Journal on this.

Wave Four

Embody your Soul Purpose

Tune into your inner wisdom, and ignite the light within

to be who you were born to be. Using prayer, meditation,

contemplation and your own inner guidance, you can tune

into the coconut wireless of the cosmos and Universal

Love.

"The Path to God is a simple one of Joy."

Hawaiian Proverb

"What starts as an outward search always ends up as an uncovering of something that existed with us all along."

Pila of Hawaii

My journey home to myself began with searching far and wide outside myself for external gratification, external rewards, acceptance of others and a mask of happiness. I took the long way round, but luckily it only took me about three decades to come home to ME. I had been there all along.

I hope this book will help you on your quest to find yourself and return home to turn on and tune in, awakening the light within you. BEcome one with the The Universe, God, Universal LOVE because it's the Universe that really does have your back.

We can get so busy being busy in our lives. We get dogs that we pay someone else to walk, we have our phones on us at all times, we watch reality TV looking for inspiration, we swipe right or left looking for connections, we rink to celebrate, we drink to commiserate, we fill the void with addictions to food, drink, drugs, exercise and work. And still, we don't feel whole.

What are your thoughts on this?

A Peaceful Practise

What if the only thing missing is YOU?
Journal on this thought, or sit in stillness,
and let inspiration come.

*"What is the greatest lesson
a woman should learn?*

*That since day one, she's already had
everything she needs within herself. It's the
world that convinced her she did not."*

Rupi Kaur

A Peaceful Practise

Envision the life you want!
What gifts do you have that already serves this purpose?
What gifts do you have already within you?
Amplify them!

What no longer serves this purpose?
Let it go.

"There is a voice that doesn't use words. Listen."

Rumi

BE still.
BE quiet.
LISTEN to your intuition.

Peaceful Practises help you BE!

Music is not made up of the individual notes but of the spaces between the notes. That's where the magic is.

Your own innate knowing—your intuition—is there in the silence. Listen!

So often, our minds are so busy that we can't hear ourselves think.
Drop down out of your head and into your HEART SPACE.
Breathe, BE Still and Listen.

In this SPACE,
we connect to Our Inner Knowing,
our Inner Guidance System,
our Inner wisdom,
our Intuition,
The Divine,
Our Higher Self
and Universal Love.

"Want to save the world?

Do what you love!

Find your path!

Life is too short,

too precious to spend your days

out of synch with your own heart."

Waylon H. Lewis

*"If prayer is you talking to God, then intuition
is God talking to you."*

Wayne Dyer

Intuition

Connect to your own Inner Guidance, Your Compass.

Feel into your True North—Your Truth!

Have Faith and Trust in Your connection to Source.

You already Know!

Your own Innate Knowing will bring you Courage.

When you absolutely know THIS and FEEL this on a SOUL level,

No one can persuade you or deter you.

No one can knock you off course.

Rather than following someone else's map and walking their path,

You are creating your own Path.

A Peaceful Practise

Pause.

Meditate.

Listen in the Silence.

You can ask a question before you begin the silence,

and you can journal afterwards.

You may Feel, hear or just know the answers you seek.

Your own truth.

Your intuition.

*"When you do things from your soul,
you feel a river moving in you, a Joy."*

Rumi

Am I on the right path?
Trust.
Have faith.
Believe.

How do you know you are on the right path, going in the right direction?
What signs do you see that encourage and inspire you?
Notice recurring patterns, numbers, images and animals.

Butterflies are inspirational. The transformation they go through from caterpillar to cocoon to chrysalis to butterfly is a great metaphor for what we humans experience.

Where are you on your journey?

For me, butterflies are a sign from the universe and from my mum (together) that I am not alone and I am going in the right direction.

When my mum passed away three years ago, I saw butterflies everywhere, even though it was winter. They would fly with me as I walked my dogs. I always say, "Hello, Mum" when I see them, whether it's on a mountaintop in Nepal or in an image in a magazine. All are signs to me.

These signs are real!
Have Faith.
Trust.
Believe.
Know.

A Peaceful Practise

What recurring signs do you notice?
What do you see as signs from the Universe?
What gives you inspiration and reassures you?
Do you ignore them, or are you curious about them?
Start to pay attention to recurring numbers,
images that keep popping up,
a song on the radio that happens to
have the words you needed to hear.
Do you notice words on signs in the subway
or on the street that stand out to you?
What do you notice?
Open up to noticing more,
and there will be.

Let's say you are trying to decide between doing something or not doing it.

This is your conundrum.

You are going to weigh the options of each decision.

1.   First, stand with your feet firmly planted on the ground. This is wonderful to do outside where you can connect directly to the earth's energy. You are tuning your own compass.

2.   Close your eyes, and breathe calmly in through your nose and out through your mouth. (Yes, you know this is my go-to suggestion for breathing.) Feel yourself calming down, slowing down and becoming more present in your body. Notice how you feel.

3.   We want to find out what a Yes or No feels like.

4.   Now, ask yourself a simple Truth like "Is my name (your real name)?" or "Is my favourite colour (your actual favourite colour)?" How does this feel? Notice how you stand or sway. Pay attention to how your shoulders, stomach and head feel. You may notice you sway forward, back or to one side. This is how the Truth, a positive "YES" feels for you in your body. If you don't like your name, however, don't use this. Make sure it's something you feel positive about so you don't get a false positive. You can quite simply say, "YES" when you answer the question.

5. Open your eyes. Notice something external to you—maybe a tree, the sky or a bird singing.

6. Now, close your eyes again. Breathe calmly again as above. This time, ask yourself a question with a Negative answer. "Is my name (not your real name)?" or "Is my favourite colour (not your actual favourite colour)?" Feel what this feels like. Notice what's different about your body. Notice where the energy has shifted. How do your stomach, shoulders and head feel? Maybe you feel an ache somewhere. Maybe you sway back, to the side or forward. This is how a negative—a lie, a "NO"—feels in your body.

7. Now that you have a sense of what YES/Positive versus NO/Negative feels like, you can move on to your conundrum.

8. Close your eyes, breathe calmly as above, and when you feel grounded, picture option one. Visualise yourself doing the "thing" that is the first of your choices. Feel what it would feel like, or say whatever it is, repeating it. Then, do the same for the second of your two choices.

9. Your body should feel differently between the two options. If you don't feel any difference, it could be a neutral choice with no clear right or wrong.

10. You can do this for something with more than two options as well.

> *"Don't look for your Dreams to become True;*
> *look to become True to Your Dreams."*

Michael Beckwith

Read that again!

What does this mean to you?

Who do you need to Be for your Dreams to come True?

Where do you need to Grow?

What do you need to let go?

Where are you in alignment with your Dreams?

For me, it's about BE-coming the person of the Dream.

A Peaceful Practise

Meditate on these questions, and listen.

Try writing in free flow in response to these questions.

Don't analyse or edit; just let the words flow.

Michael Beckwith has an amazing process called "Life Visioning".
I highly recommend you try it.

Choose LOVE

Have you walked into a room and felt the vibe drag you down?

You get to choose the vibe!
So choose LOVE.

This will raise up the vibration—the feeling in the room.
You get to raise the vibe rather than having it drag you down.

You can also choose to leave the room! No one said you had to stay there.

A Peaceful Practise

Just breathe and
feel LOVE in your heart.
Drop down out of your head into your heart.
BREATHE.
Feel how you want to FEEL.
Feel it in your HEART.
Inhale . . . exhale.
Feel the feeling, and let it grow and RADIATE
out into the room and beyond.

Protection Energy Bubble

We can protect ourselves from negative vibes and other people's vibes.
Close your eyes.
If you aren't somewhere you feel comfortable doing this, focus your
mind's eye inwards on the next blink.

Take three deep breaths in through your nose and out through your
mouth.
Imagine a white, loving light from above streaming down upon you like a
waterfall.
Feel the pure loving energy flowing down and around you completely,
circling you like a Giant Bubble.
This bubble of light is your sacred space.
You are holding space for yourself.
You are Safe.
You are Love.
This is your Energy Bubble.
Feel Safe.
Feel Love.

Say "**Bubble**" or "**I command my sacred space.**"

A Peaceful Practise

You can make the bubble a colour of your choice.

I like pink, purple, green or golden light

Protection Bubble (Activation)

I use this for my car, and the first time I KNEW it worked was when
I was driving down a five-lane freeway in Texas and literally drove
right through the middle of cars jackknifing around me. It was a weird
moment as I observed this, holding on to the steering wheel as I left the
accident behind me. I said, "Thank you, Jesus."

There as a huge truck to my right, and the driver glanced over at me
with a startled look on his face, mouthing the words, "Are you okay?"
You could see the bemusement on his face, having witnessed me driving
through without a scratch on me or my car.

Before turning on your car, close your eyes.
Breathe into your heart.
Imagine you see each of the four corners of your car.
Imagine a beautiful bubble of healing light surrounding you and
protecting you,
circling all four corners,
above and below.
Trust that you are safe.
Trust that you are love and protected.
Drive safely.

A Peaceful Practise

On times I've forgotten to do this, as soon as I remember,
I just say "Bubble" as I keep my eyes on the road,
getting a sense of the bubble of protection
encompassing all four corners, above and below the car.

"There must be something strangely sacred in salt.
It is in our tears and in the sea."

Kahlil Gibran

I am drawn to the sea, as it nourishes my Soul.

I just know that I feel at peace and happy by the ocean.

Where do you go to nourish your SOUL?

A Peaceful Practise

Journal about where you FEEL most Peaceful,

Happy.

Inspired.

Feel the feelings of being there.

*"The ocean stirs the heart, inspires the imagination
and brings eternal joy to the soul."*

Robert Wyland

Your Dream Location

Where do you love to BE?
What place feeds your Heart and Soul?

Even though I live near the sea, I don't have a view of it. It's my dream to
live with a view of the ocean from my home so that I can drink my
morning coffee and be mesmerised by the ever-changing motion of the
waves.

A Peaceful Practise

Visualise your Dream location, real or imagined.
Feel the feelings of being there as if you are.
Notice what you notice.
Hear, See, Feel, Taste, Sense.
You can hold this vision for as long as you like.
Feel this with your Heart, Body and Soul.
How do you feel whilst doing this and afterwards?

Hakalau

Hakalau is an ancient Hawaiian practise that expands your awareness in the present moment. There are no distractions of negative emotions—only awareness in the present moment.

Hakalau is believed to improve your concentration, the use of your senses, your ability to learn, and your overall performance.

A Peaceful Practise

Gaze in front of you.
Gently soften your focus, becoming aware of your peripheral vision.
It can help to focus on a spot on the wall or in the distance.

Try raising your hands directly in front of you in the "thumbs up" position.
Look at your thumbs.

Keep your gaze forward, and move your arms out in front of you, then out
to your sides as far as you can still see your thumbs in your peripheral vision.
You can drop your hands to your sides or keep them up to the sides.
Hold your softened gaze forward.
You will find over time that your peripheral vision increases.
Notice if you become aware of your other senses improving.
What do you notice?

I do this on some of my walks.
As a result, I become more aware of the sounds happening around me.
I have a different awareness of my surroundings.
However, please be careful doing this while walking,

"And one day she discovered that she was fierce, and strong, and full of fire, and that not even she could hold herself back because her passion burned brighter than her fears."

Mark Anthony

How DO YOU show up in life every day?
Are you a Co-Creator and Leader in your own life?
Are you showing up fully and completely in your life with total self-acceptance?

What is leadership?
What is success?
Think about it.

Let's go a little deeper and get to where the magic is beyond the automatic responses.

For me, leadership and success are in small meaningful and inspiring actions, heartFULLness, kindness, and the simple day-to-day things we do. Like helping your child with their homework and Being fully present with them as you do.

Holding space for your client to have that "ah ha" moment of clarity and transformation.

Smiling at a stranger and feeling content whether they smile back or not.

A Peaceful Practise

What is success to you?

Think about this beyond the surface.

Go deeper.

Pause.

Listen.

Your mind believes everything you tell it!
Fill it with LOVE!

unknown*

We have touched on the law of attraction without calling it Law of
Attraction (LOA):
Like attracts like.
Like finds like.
Where our attention goes, energy flows.
What you resist persists.
I've asked you to consider the FEELs, the Whys and to go deeper on
your intentions and desires.
I have also suggested you trust and have faith in the Universe.

Do you want to know how manifestation works?
We are mostly unaware of our true level of Desire or our true level of
Resistance to what we want to Manifest.
We need to drop our resistance to what we Desire to Manifest!

Manifestation = Desire minus Resistance (M= D-R)
What is it you claim to Desire (D)?
How bad do you want it? What is your Resistance (R) to it?

What you Desire to create, co-create and bring into being is in
opposition to your RESISTANCE.

Here's an example: My gran never bought a lottery ticket because she knew without a shadow of a doubt that she would win, and she wanted people who needed the money more to win. She trusted and believed this to be true. She also had some facts: She won every raffle she ever entered. She didn't question the chances of her winning. To her, the odds of her winning were 100% in her favour.

Bethal, on the other hand is someone I knew who brought a lottery ticket every week, sure that she'd win. She felt so close. She was positive, she was optimistic, she expressed her desire to win and expressed what she'd do with the winnings. BUT here is the RESISTANCE: When asked her chances of winning, she said, "Oh, well, the likes of me never wins." BOOM! There you have it! When I asked her to delve deeper, her resistance was about 90%, so the odds were not in her favour.

A Peaceful Practise

What Resistance do you have to what you Desire?
Journal about your Resistance.
Listen.
Then, commit to dropping the Resistance to
what YOU want!

Relax—

Nothing
is
under
Control.

Control is an illusion.

The harder you try to control,
The harder life can feel,
The more frazzled we feel.
In fact, it gets freaking exhausting.

It's so tiring when we try to control our lives.

Relax . . .
Do what you can to create the life you want
and live in joy from moment to moment . . .
Then, trust in the process.
Go with the Flow.

Being in Flow
Feels Easy—
like paddling with the currant of the stream
rather than fighting upstream.

"Water is the softest thing, yet it can penetrate mountains and earth. This shows clearly the principle of softness overcoming hardness."

Lao Zi

A Peaceful Practise

Where in your life can you soften your focus?

"Many people think excitement

is happiness . . .

But when you are excited,

you are not peaceful.

True happiness is based on peace."

Thich Nhat Hanh

"Looking behind,
I am filled with gratitude,
looking forward,
I am filled with vision,
looking upwards I am filled with strength,
looking within, I discover peace."

Quero Apache Prayer

A Peaceful Practise

Meditate on this.

The Full Abundance Change me Prayer

by Tosha Silver from *It's Not Your Money*

This is my favourite abundance prayer. I casually recite the last five lines when I feel inspired. I love the idea of releasing what no longer serves the higher good of all and my purpose, while calling in what is needed for abundance to come in. It's like clearing out a junk drawer.

Divine Beloved, Allow me to give with complete ease and abundance, knowing that You are the unlimited Source of All.

Let me be an easy open conduit for Your prosperity.
Let me trust that all of my own needs are always met in amazing ways and it's safe to give freely as my heart guides.

And equally, please let me feel wildly open to receiving.

May I know my own value, beauty and worthiness without question.
Let me allow others the supreme pleasure of giving to me.
May I feel worthy to receive in every possible way.

And let me extend kindness to all who need, feeling compassion and understanding in even the hardest situations.

Change me into One who can fully love, forgive,
and accept myself . . . so I may carry your Light without restriction.

Let everything that needs to go, go.
Let everything that needs to come, come.
I am utterly Your own.

You are Me, I am You, We are One.
All is well.

A Peaceful Practise

Say this prayer every day for 40 days.
I have it taped to my mirror to read every
morning when getting ready for my day.

"I no longer force things. What flows, flows. What crashes, crashes. I only have space and energy for things that are meant for me."

Billy Chapata

Are you willing to navigate the waves of change as they come?
To ride the waves?
To trust and have faith?
To Be present?

Can you let go of your expectations?

Are you willing to Let Go, Let God (Source/the Universe)?

Let Go, and Find your way home!

A Peaceful Practise

Breathe.

Let Go.

"Your healing lifts up the whole ocean of existence.
When you heal we all heal."

Yung Pueblo

One Love

One person at a time

One mind at a time

One heart at a time

One day at a time

We are all connected

Oneness

Together we heal

Together we rise

One Love

A Peaceful Practise

Meditate on the word Love.

The Voyage Home

"If Light is in your Heart, you will find your way home."

Rumi

It has been my intention with this book to take you on a voyage of self-reflection and self-discovery. I don't know what treasures you will find on your journey through these pages.

Use what works for you or inspires you, and try the daily practises that speak to you. This book will be here for you to dip in and out of for inspiration, should you need it.

Navigate the ocean of life in a way that is unique to you, awaken your light within and live with ease, grace and authenticity.

I wish you well on your journey of discovery to Your Soul Purpose and Your True North.

With love,

Iona

For examples of daily routines and rituals that I like, pop over to the
bonus page at https://ionarussell.com/making-waves-bonus-material/

*There are BONUS materials available on my website for you to download,
including meditations, PDF's, journal prompts and more. I will continue to
add to this over time as I am inspired to create more.*
https://ionarussell.com/making-waves-bonus-material/

Acknowledgements

The list is long, and I am humbled to have these beautiful souls as part of my soul family.

I would like to start off by thanking my birth family, and in particular my mum, Maggie, who always believed in me and supported all my spirited and rebellious choices.

My son, Callum, for putting up with my odd hours, being there through the shouty mum stage and the unfolding of this journey across seas, mountains and finding our Zen home.

To my brothers, Kyle and Martin, thank you for always keeping it real and making me laugh a lot. Extra appreciation to my sister-in-laws, Kristen and Christa—you each bring such vitality and strength to this family. I love all your children (Freya, Gwenny, Kael and Morgan) as if they were my own. I'm so grateful to you all for being there with our mum all the way through to the end. I'm blessed to have you as my brothers and sisters.

Thank you to my dad, Kurt, for your patience in teaching me to paint and see the wonder in the Universe, be it a view from the Gompa or the shades of purple in a cabbage on the kitchen table.

I am indebted to The Aunts, Cecilia, Judy and Mary, for being there through the years and supporting me without judgement, having me to stay, helping with Callum and sharing all those fond memories of Rossie and my mum. To ALL my cousins for your support and laughter, and all the family near and far.

Jerry-Pops, Nina and Alexis, I thank Mum for bringing you into my life. Alexis for being my sister in every sense of the word. Nina for supporting and encouraging me no matter where I was in my life. Pops for bringing music and laughter into our house.

Moving on to my sacred soul family, who have all played significant parts in many lifetimes:

So much gratitude to Madhavi Kata Chalasani, the energy medicine and shamanic healer of Chakra Bliss Center https://chakrablisscenter.com/, who has been pivotal in guiding me home to myself and the Divine.

Kristi, who taught me so much about grounding, introduced me to "The work of Byron Katie", and for joining me in Austin for our first Hay House event. To Pam, who was instrumental in Dragon Fly meetings and out-of-the-box thinking; I miss our lunch time conversations over soup and fancy tea.

To all my friends who have supported me in Texas during my journey through "Tears at Midnight" to divorce and leaving your shores, you are all important and hold a special place in my heart. Shazzia and her family, for being there through thick and thin with lots of adventures, black diamond skiing and wild sailing; and thank you for all those evening gatherings with laughter, conversation and music. Lisa and The Q's for helping out with soccer runs, cruises and cake extravaganzas. Tiffany and her family for having us as part of their family and for loving my gingerbread cookies … with laughter.

Melissa, for our cul-du-sac conversations about adoption and adventures, travel and tacos; Stacey, watching our kids grow together in the early years, with skateboards and wall ball; Beth, Shannon and Susan, thank you for our "walk 'n talk" mornings, which were such a monumental support for me; Beth, thank you for that chips and Diet Coke lunch where you held my hand as I cried my marriage away; Rebecca, thank you for not letting me cut my hair, our coffee chats and for always being supportive no matter what was going on; Patti, you were like my mama there at CASA and a dear friend outside of work. Thank you for your unwavering support and encouragement, even when I didn't believe in myself. I'd never have lasted at CASA without your encouragement.

Luke, you are the most amazing young man, and I am blessed that you came into my life with your huge heart and sense of humour. To all the jokes we shared, to your life with your family, Sophia, Sandra and Doug, and all the success that is yours to have.

Warmest thanks to all those on this book journey with me for their unwavering support and belief. Sean Patrick, my publisher at That Guys House, for believing in my story. Karen Mills-Alston, for her support. Tanya Arler and that chance encounter that started a chain of unexpected events. Sarah Lloyd, Indigo Soul PR, for getting me seen, seeing the potential in me and being a friend who goes above and beyond. Thank you to Melanie Votaw for her editing in creating flow and making everything make more sense than it did.

Huge "shout out loud" gratitude to David Hamilton, who called me an author before I was ready to myself: who said a year before I even signed my publishing deal that I was a shining star with great things ahead of me after looking at my Mandala in Tanya Arler's workshop in London. This was the same workshop where he brought tears to my eyes when he shared stories from his soul about his dog and about deodorant falling out of the sky. So much gratitude to David for writing such a heartfelt endorsement for this book. Thank you!

Michelle St.Onge for being a sister over the years, for always being there even when we had a tick infestation, and for all the ways you have inspired me with your art. Thank you Michelle St.Onge for your "Heartfelt Gift" that is the cover of this book. You have added a depth of Heart and Soul with your intuitive creative genius, which resonates to it's core. Check her out at www. michellesaintonge.com/
Thank you!

Nigel for taking me on an adventure and seeing me through to BE Zen Iona.

OrlaithB, your business coaching and friendship is an ongoing support. Thank you for pushing me to go further than I dreamed possible with my business and all my creations.

Aloha. Jane Wardlaw, Hugh Gilbert and the KCR family, "The Hawaii KCR Tribe", "The Ohana Circle" and Sally for all those walks and talks on the beach in Hawaii. Darren for your support, walking labyrinths and sharing chocolate. Harry Uhane Jim, Thank you!

There are no words except "Thank you and I Love you" to Jennie, Jesus, Lori, Jeremiah, Melissa, Brian and Brian. Spiritual Soul Family to the core. Brian Cashman "Thank you" for your diligent note taking.

Thank you to everyone of the BEautiful soul SiSTARS who are part of Jodee's Teepee Weekender. Deepest gratitude to Jodee Peevor, for seeing what I do before I did. Karina Ladet for teaching me to deepen my listening and intuition. Carolyn Flower for taking me further on the book journey than I could have managed without you. I appreciate your intuitive guidance and reaching out to me before we even met. Abby Wilkes for your special photographs that see the Soul Essence. Iris for all our ice cream conversations in London. Kindred Souls.

Sarah Lloyd, Indigo Soul PR, for your EPIC intuitive guidance, "Alchemy" sessions and so much love and laughter along our journey together (even at midnight).

Amber Valdez, Life Purpose Cheerleader, for helping me to turn up my light and live on purpose, unapologetically. Patty for being part of the journey with heart and soul.

Cathy Wilke, Freedom and Fulfillment Business Coaching, for your unwavering support, patience and for holding space for me, above and beyond the call of duty.

Tara for saying how it is, being the Wild Witchy Woman of the North, naming "Holding Space" (my upcoming book) and for sharing in the vision from the beginning. Our morning coffees and conversations have been educational. Lesley for helping me to sort out my overloaded vortex of ideas into "that" ah-ha moment over coffee. Alison for her unwavering faith in me. I miss your face. Sarah for all your support over the decades, your humour and your honesty. Kate for looking after my house and dogs so I could go on adventures to grow and evolve with my business and in creating this book. Guri for pizza nights and deep conversations. Ditte for teaching me to relax and enjoy photoshoots and for bringing me out of my shell. Mel for releasing the dragons. Gail for all those late night dancing sessions and support. Mitch, Kerry, Andy, Leigh, Jools, Adrian, Julie, Jeremy, Wee Lynne (for our philosophical conversations), Craig and Janine for wild camping, groovy dancing and lots of adventures. Pete for being there for Callum.

Last, but by no means least, to some of the siSTARS who have known me the longest and are still part of my life. Lesley, what can I say except thank you for still being my friend even after you got "that" tattoo and for all your encouragement over the years. Cheryl, we were sisters before we even met, and you know that's the truth. I love you.

Let's not forget where I came from—thanks to the 2 Sally's and Amanda: thank you for always being full of laughter. Jane, "thank you" for that song. Lauren for finding me after so many years with Meredith, Kendra, Dave, Sean and the old Boulder crew, too.

Nothing is accomplished alone; it takes a village, as they say. There are so many more beautiful souls I could mention here, but then the thank yous would become longer than the book. Please know I have not intentionally left anyone out. I am sure I have forgotten someone and will wish I'd named you when this book is in production. Please know that everyone I've met in this life time, I appreciate you, as you have all contributed to who I am today.

Thank you!

I Love You!

About the Author

Iona Russel is certified in Clinical Hypnotherapy (Dip.C.Hyp), Past Life Regression (PLR), Neuro-linguistic Programming (NLP), Kinetic Chain Release (KCR Masters), Advanced Ho'oponopono and Postural Energetics and Life Coaching. She is a challenger of change and spiritual catalyst. Her core philosophy is that no matter who you are, where you're from or your personal circumstances, it is possible to reinvent yourself from the inside out and live the life you were born to live. We all have innate wellbeing, health and happiness within us. Iona has proven her own philosophy many times over by overcoming personal struggles with depression, stress and confidence. She believes everyone can get out of their "funk" and flow to a place of purpose, passion and joy.

In Polynesian cultures, a Wayfinder intuitively understands the environment and the elements, plotting the course for their own lives and for others across the oceans. Iona Russell is your Wayfinder, who helps you to find your true north while navigating you towards discovering your hidden treasures—your soul purpose, your dharma, your inner light. She guides you to discover authentic happiness and success in your life.

Learn more about her Private and Group Coaching Programs at
www.ionarussell.com

The following are correct at the time of printing.

Group Coaching Programs

Ignite Your Purpose Immersion. The world is dire need of people who have woken up to their spiritual and energetic gifts. Uncover your gifts and bring them into the light on this personal pilgrimage of self-discovery with Iona Russell. Learn how to harness your energetic gifts to be a contribution to others and to the world.

Shine Your Light Without Fear or Hesitation. The world needs you and it needs your work. In this deep dive with Iona Russell, you will tune into the soul of your business where you will release the thoughts and fears that are keeping you stuck and hiding. You will dismantle the mask of who you think you should be in your business so that you can be who you truly are.

Private Life Coaching Programs

1-1 VIP Soulpreneurs Breakthrough - *Free Your Mind Accelerator & ReBoost Process* for Creatives, Healers and Soulpreneurs* (or those who aspire to be). Release blocks and embrace your purpose with Iona's guidance and expertise.

*A soulpreneur is an entrepreneur, freelancer, artist, craftsperson, coach or anyone else who looks at life and business as an opportunity for expression of their higher self. Successful Soulpreneurs are defined more by their approach to life than by the type of work they are doing.

1-1 Wayfinder Coaching Program - *Discover Your True North Treasure.* Bespoke packages to navigate your soul journey.

Learn more about her Private and Group Coaching Programs at **www.ionarussell.com**

Upcoming Books

Making Waves: The Workbook will be uniquely designed as a companion to this book.

Holding Space is part memoir, part self-help. Join Iona on her journey of change and transformation.

Endnotes and References

Introduction

"**Last Night a D.J. Saved My Life**" is a song written by Michael Cleveland for American group Indeep. It features vocals from Réjane "Reggie" Magloire and Rose Marie Ramsey. Recorded in 1981 and release February 15 1982 under the label Sound of New York/ Becket Records, produced by Mike Cleveland, Reggie Thompson

Wayne Dyer, *The Power of Intention* "Change The Way You Look At Things, And The Things You Look At Change" Hay House UK Limited, 2004

WAVE ONE
Harry Uhane Jim, Garnette Arledge Wise Secrets of Aloha: Learn and Live the Sacred Art of Lomilomi, p.145 **"This breathing is intended to enjoin the presence of the verb of God to heal through emotional evolution."** Harry Uhane Jim, Weiser Books, 1 Mar 2007

Gary Zukav books include "*The Seat Of The Soul*" (Random House, 31 Dec 2012), *"Soul Stories*" (Gary Zukav, Linda Francis Simon and Schuster, 11 Dec 2012) and "*The HEart of the Soul*" (Gary Zukav, Linda Francis Simon and Schuster, 11 Dec 2012), this quote appears on the internet at
https://www.goodreads.com/quotes/7292709-you-cannot-find-your-soul-with-your-mind-you-must
"You cannot find your soul with your mind, You must use your heart. You must

know what you are feeling. If you don't know what you are feeling, you will create unconsciously. If you are unconscious of an aspect of yourself; if it operates outside your field of awareness, that aspect has power over you."

Elizabeth Gilbert, *Eat Pray Love: One Woman's Search for Everything*, p.28, **"To find the balance you want, this is what you must become. You must keep your feet grounded so firmly on the earth that it's like you have four legs instead of two. That way, you can stay in the world. But you must stop looking at the world through your head. You must look through your heart, instead. That way, you will know God."**, Bloomsbury Publishing, 16 Nov 2009

Gill Hasson, *Mindfulness Pocketbook: Little Exercises for a Calmer Life*, p.14 references Thich Nhat Hanh "Feelings come and go like clouds in a windy sky. Conscious breathing is my anchor." John Wiley & Sons, 13 Apr 2015

Eckhart Tolle, *The Power of Now: A Guide to Spiritual Enlightenment*, p.154 **"To know yourself as the Being underneath the thinker, the stillness underneath the mental noise, the love and joy underneath the pain, is freedom, salvation, enlightenment." New World Library, 6 Oct 2010**

Richard Bach, *Jonathan Livingston Seagull: T*he Complete Edition, p.26 **"Jonathan Seagull discovered that boredom and fear and anger are the reasons that a gull's life is so short, and with these gone from his thought, he lived a long fine life indeed." Simon and Schuster, 21 Oct 2014**

Alain & Jody Herriott, have developed 'The Wonder Method' **https://thewondermethod.com/** and written *Energy Healing and the Art of Awakening through*

Wonder, Herriott, Herriot, and Odysseus, 30 Sep 2016

This quote appears on their website - **"Within us is a tumultuous ocean of feeling. When we are caught in these currents of mental unrest, all we see is conflict. Through feeling those feelings and allowing them to unwind we return to calmness."**

Larry Chang, *Wisdom for the Soul: Five Millennia of Prescriptions for Spiritual Healing,* p.463

"We can only BE what we give ourselves the Power to BE!" cherokee saying, Gnosophia Publishers, 2006

Darryl Anka,or Albert Einstein who is generally credited with, **"Everything is energy, Match the frequency of the reality you want, and you cannot help but get that reality."** but there is no definitive proof of this. There are a number of websites that debate this including https://quoteinvestigator.com/2012/05/16/everything-energy/, where it is generally attributed to Darryl Anka, who channels Bashar. If you google Darryl Anka, Bashar you will find the quote on websites such as these https://www.goodreads.com/ quotes/571191-everything-is-energy-and-that-s-all-there-is-to-it https://truthloveunity. wordpress.com/2014/03/26/bashar-quotes/ , http://www.lightascension.com/arts/ wise%20words2.htm

"like attracts like" is a term frequently used in writings on The Law of Attraction. To quote the author Richard Bach who wrote 'Jonathan Livingston Seagull', and 'Illusions: The Adventures of a Reluctant Messiah' *(Dell Publishing Co., Inc. 1977)* who is quoted in Beyond Words: *Terms for Transforming Consciousness, p.134 saying* **"Like attracts like. Just be who you are, calm and clear and bright."** Harbin Springs Pub., 1990

Gillian Anderson and Jennifer Nadel, We: A Manifesto for Women Everywhere, p.8 quotes

Alice Walker "Thank you' is the best prayer that anyone could say. I say that one a lot. **Thank you expresses extreme gratitude, humility, understanding."** Simon and Schuster, 7 Mar 2017

David R. Hamilton, PHD, *How Your Mind Can Heal Your Body: 10th Anniversary Edition*, p160 quotes **"Happiness cannot be traveled to, owned, earned, worn or consumed. Happiness is the spiritual experience of living every minute with love, grace, and gratitude."** by Denis Waitley. Hay House, Inc, 1 Feb 2010

Marianne Williamson, article *What You Think Is What You Get-* **From the September 2000 issue of** O, The Oprah Magazine**.** I discovered the article online at http://www.oprah.com/spirit/marianne-williamson-what-you-think-is-what-you-get **"In the realm of thought, there are two main categories: thoughts of love and thoughts of fear. Every single moment, we choose between the two. If I think with love, then I am more likely to behave lovingly and to attract love from others. If my heart is closed, I am more likely to act out of fear. Fear-based behavior tends not to look like fear but like anger or jealousy; it elicits reactions from others that reflect my fear and not my love."**

Thich Nhat Hanh, **"At any moment, you have a choice, that either leads you closer to your spirit or further away from it."** https://www.goodreads.com/quotes/376441-at-any-moment-you-have-a-choice-that-either-leads

Dodinsky, *In the Garden of Thoughts,* **"Do not become a stranger to yourself by blending."** Sourcebooks, Inc., 16 Apr 2013. I found this quote online at **https://www. goodreads.com/quotes/829038-do-not-become-a-stranger-to-yourself-by-blending-in**

Denis Waitley, https://www.goodreads.com/author/quotes/5108.Denis_Waitley
"It's not who you are that holds you back; it's who you THINK you are not that holds you back!"
Stephen Galloza, Faith, Hope, & Psychology, The Miracle Zone, "80 % of Thoughts Are Negative...95 % are repetitive", published March 2, 2012, and stating that 'In 2005, the National Science Foundation published an article regarding research about human thoughts per day. The average person has about 12,000 to 60,000 thoughts per day. Of those, 80% are negative and 95% are exactly the same repetitive thoughts as the day before and about 80% are negative. " https://faithhopeandpsychology.wordpress.com/2012/03/02/80-of-thoughts-are-negative-95-are-repetitive/

Thich Nhat Hanh, **"Sometimes your joy is the source of your smile, but sometimes your smile can be the source of your joy."** appears in
https://www.goodreads.com/quotes/7704-sometimes-your-joy-is-the-source-of-your-smile-but. According to quote catalog h**ttps://quotecatalog.com/quote/ga4VmK7/**
"Quote not verified; source unknown"

Considered an Irish blessing or toast, original source unknown, **"May Your Joys Be As Deep As the Ocean."** It is listed in many toasting books aimed at celebrations and ceremony's.

Germany Kent, books include The Hope Handbook: *The Search for Personal Growth.* Amazon Digital Services LLC - Kdp Print Us, 14 Mar 2015, and The Hope Handbook for Mentors and Coaches: *The Search for Personal Growth.* Star Stone Press, 17 Apr 2015. She is listed as a strategic thinker at https://www.goodreads.com/quotes/tag/strategic-thinking **"Learn to master your thoughts and watch closely what you deposit into your spirit. Speak over your life. Living in peace has transformative power."**

Mhairi Scott, *An Angelic Toolkit for the Spiritual Traveller*, p.179 **"Many people think excitement is happiness... But when you are excited you are not peaceful. True happiness is based on peace. "** -Thich Nhat Hanh. Balboa Press, 4 Jun 2013. According to 'Medivate'
 http://medivate.com/quote/126/thich-nhat-hanh/many-people-think-excitement-is/ the original source is Thich Nhat Hanh, The Art of Power, Harper Collins, 13 Oct 2009.

WAVE TWO

Wayne Dyer. AZQuotes.com, Wind and Fly LTD, 2019. https://www.azquotes.com/quote/877805 , accessed October 06, 2019. **"If you don't make peace with your past, it will keep showing up in your present."**

The 'Aloha KCR family', are the amazing group of wisdom seekers and "Kinetic Chain Release" practitioners, that I was with in Hawaii 2018 for the first Master's level, led by Hugh Gilbert and Jane Wardlaw. You can find out more about "Kinetic Chain Release"at https://www.kineticchainrelease.com/ We had the pleasure to spend a day together learning from Harry Uhane Jim.

Harry Uhane Jim, *Wise Secrets of Aloha: Talk Story with Hawaiian Healer, Harry Uhane Jim,* May 2016 - September 2016. This Ho'oponopono prayer is quoted from the series at https://vimeo.com/search/ondemand?q=wise+secrets+of+aloha
I wish to credit my dear friend **Brian Cashman** and fellow Aloha traveller for sharing his notes, on this valuable series. I first learnt about *Harry Uhane Jim from the book co written with* , Garnette Arledge, Wise Secrets of Aloha: *Learn and Live the*

Sacred Art of Lomilomi." Weiser Books, 1 Mar 2007 "Harry Uhane Jim is one of the last Kahuna of Lomilomi, Keeper of the Deep Mysteries of authentic Hawaiian esoterica. He shares the secrets of this ancient oral tradition with readers for the first time in Wise Secrets of Aloha. Recognizing that the world is in great peril, Kahuna Harry was blessed by the Halau Guardians who instructed him to share the true teachings and tools of Lomilomi for the practice of physical, emotional, and spiritual healing. He writes: "Now is the time to share aloha with humanity. `Aloha' means the Breath of God is in our Presence. It is time to reveal the profound Lomilomi secrets of the kahunas for personal and planetary peace." Wise Secrets of Aloha is as simple as it is profound, as contemporary as it is ancient. It is true to Hawaiian esoteric teachings and available to all who bring the right attitude. Aloha calls. Listen in the splash of waves, in the breeze-- the air is filled with aloha. All the abundance, joy, and freedom from old wounds readers have ever yearned for can be found by adopting the aloha spirit." This is quoted from https://books.google.co.uk/books?id=NHVssdwJxDoC&dq=ho%27oponopono+harry+uhane+jim&source=gbs_navlinks_s You can learn more about Harry Uhane Jim at http://harryjimlomilomi.com/10385.html , http://harryjimlomilomi.com/209926.html

"Everything is energy. Your thought begins it, your emotion amplifies it and your action increases the momentum." (unknown). My favourite exploration of this is written by Evelyn Lim Thought-Emotion-Action for Manifestation https://www.evelynlim.com/thought-emotion-action-for-manifestation/ April 27, 2015

John Lennon, *"Celebrating John Lennon's Birthday in His Own Inspiring Words" by Jeryl Brunner, parade.com. October 09, 2014* https://parade.com/345465/jerylbrunner/celebrating-john-lennons-birthday-in-his-own-inspiring-words/
"John Lennon." AZQuotes.com. Wind and Fly LTD, 2019. 06 October 2019.

https://www.azquotes.com/quote/351036

Byron Katie, AZQuotes.com, Wind and Fly LTD, 2019. https://www.azquotes.com/ quote/377992, accessed October 06, 2019. **"Placing the blame or judgment on someone else leaves you powerless to change your experience; taking responsibility for your beliefs and judgments gives you the power to change them."**

Maya Angelou. AZQuotes.com, Wind and Fly LTD, 2019. https://www.azquotes.com/ quote/343701, accessed October 06, 2019. **"Success is liking yourself and liking what you do and how you do it."**

Confucius. AZQuotes.com, Wind and Fly LTD, 2019. https://www.azquotes.com/ quote/62139, accessed October 06, 2019. **"Wherever you go, go with all your heart."**

Marianne Williamson, *A Return to Love: Reflections on the Principles of A Course in Miracles*, p. 165 HarperCollins UK, 1996.

Yung Pueblo, *Inward*. Andrews McMeel Publishing, 25 Sep 2018. Twitter **Yung Pueblo** @YungPueblo 7 Nov 2016 **"True power is living the realization that you are your own healer, hero, and leader."**

C. JoyBell C. has authored books of poetry and literature that delve mainly into the mysterious, the philosophical and the esoteric.https://g.co/kgs/ZZx5dT including *The Sun Is Snowing: Poems, Parables and Pictures.* Createspace Independent Pub, 2012. This quote is noted on goodreads
https://www.goodreads.com/quotes/424700-we-can-t-be-afraid-of-change-you-may-feel-very

Haruki Murakami, *FaceBook post by Haruki Murakami from Apr 25, 2016. AZQuotes.com, Wind and Fly LTD, 2019. https://www.azquotes.com/quote/425313, accessed October 07, 2019.*

"When you come out of the storm you won't be the same person who walked in. That's what this storm's all about."

Vivian Greene, https://www.goodreads.com/author/quotes/769264.Vivian_Greene Date unknown.

"Life isn't about waiting for the storm to pass. . . . It's about learning to dance in the rain."

Yung Pueblo, *Inward*. Andrews McMeel Publishing, 25 Sep 2018. https://books.google.co.uk/

WAVE THREE

Nayyirah Waheed, *Salt*, Nayyirah Waheed, 2013.**"If the ocean can calm herself, so can you. We are all salt water mixed with air."** https://quotecatalog.com/quote/nayyirah-waheed-ifbr-the-oc-4anEgjp/

Marsha Norman. AZQuotes.com, Wind and Fly LTD, 2019. https://www.azquotes.com/author/10873-Marsha_Norman, accessed October 07, 2019.

"Dreams are illustrations. . . from the book your soul is writing about you."

KAHLIL GIBRAN, *KAHLIL GIBRAN Premium Collection: Spirits Rebellious, The Broken Wings, The Madman, Al-Nay, I Believe In You and more (Illustrated): Inspirational Books, Poetry, Spiritual Essays & Paintings of Khalil Gibran.* e-artnow, 9 Nov 2015, Inspirational Quotes section **"Trust in dreams, for in them is the hidden gate to eternity."** Jenna Galbut, **"I find it extremely liberating to see that I was the cause of all my problems. With this realization, I have also learned that I am my own solution. This is the great big gift of personal accountability. When we stop blaming external forces and own up to our responsibility, we become the ultimate creators of our destiny."** http://jennagalbut.com/index.html https://themindsjournal.com/i-find-it-extremely-liberating-to-see-that-2/

A. A. Milne. AZQuotes.com, Wind and Fly LTD, 2019. https://www.azquotes.com/quote/401051, accessed October 07, 2019.**"The things that make me different are the things that make me ME." Winnie the pooh**

Marianne Williamson *A Return to Love: Reflections on the Principles of A Course in Miracles, p.31,* **"Just like a sunbeam can't separate itself from the sun, and a wave can't separate itself from the ocean, we can't separate ourselves from one another. We are all part of a vast sea of love, one indivisible Divine mind."** Harper Collins. (2009). AZQuotes.com, Wind and Fly LTD, 2019. https://www.azquotes.com/quote/370707, accessed October 07, 2019.

Mevlana Jalaluddin Rumi, *Love's Ripening: Rumi on the Heart's Journey,* p.3 **"Wash the dust from your Soul and Heart with wisdom's Water."** Shambhala Publications, 2 Dec 2008. AZQuotes.com, Wind and Fly LTD, 2019. https://www.azquotes.com/quote/866392, accessed October 07, 2019.

Eckhart Tolle, *Twitter post from Apr 29, 2013* **"You are not separate from the whole. You are one with the sun, the earth, the air. You don't have a life. You are life."** AZQuotes. com, Wind and Fly LTD, 2019. https://www.azquotes.com/quote/499832, accessed October 07, 2019.

Harry Uhane Jim**,** Garnette Arledge, *Wise Secrets of Aloha: Learn and Live the Sacred Art of Lomilomi,* p.96 **"Hawaiian Rules",** Harry Uhane Jim, Weiser Books, 1 Mar 2007. http://harryjimlomilomi.com/10385.html
There are many who have shared their interpretation of "Kimo's Hawaian Rules"; I was particularly inspired by an article written by Philipe Borges'. https://www. motivateamazebegreat.com/2015/04/kimos-hawaiian-life-rules-to-live-by.html

WAVE FOUR

Pila of Hawaii, *The Secrets and Mysteries of Hawaii: A Call to the Soul,* p.125, **"The Path to God is a simple one of Joy."** Hawaiian Proverb. Health Communications, Incorporated, 1 Aug 1995.

Pila of Hawaii, *The Secrets and Mysteries of Hawaii: A Call to the Soul,* p.125, **"What starts as an outward search always ends up as an uncovering of something that existed with us all along."** Hawaiian Proverb. Health Communications, Incorporated, 1 Aug 1995.
Rupi Kaur, Instagram post https://www.instagram.com/p/BPi6C12AAo5/ , **"What is the greatest lesson a woman should learn? That since day one, she's already had everything she needs within herself. It's the world that convinced her she did not."** This poem is in her book *The Sun and Her Flowers,* Simon and Schuster, 3 Oct 2017

Follow her on Instagram at https://www.instagram.com/rupikaur_/ , and find out more about her on her website

Rumi, AZQuotes.com, Wind and Fly LTD, 2019. https://www.azquotes.com/quote/752096, accessed October 08, 2019. **"There is a voice that doesn't use words. Listen."**

Wayne Dyer, *Everyday Wisdom, p.36,* **"If prayer is you talking to God, then intuition is God talking to you."** *Hay House, Inc 2005. AZQuotes.com, Wind and Fly LTD, 2019. https://www.azquotes.com/quote/588863, accessed October 08, 2019.*
Waylon H. Lewis, *"Our world is full of a lot of bad news. Here's something good,"* Elephant Journal, January 8, 2018,   **"Want to save the world? Do what you love!Find your path! Life is too short, too precious to spend your days out of synch with your own heart."**

https://www.elephantjournal.com/2018/01/our-world-is-full-of-a-lot-of-bad-news-heres-something-good/
https://www.instagram.com/walkthetalkshow/?hl=en

Rumi, *'Another City'. a Selection of Poems from the Persian,* p.106 **"When you do things from your soul, you feel a river moving in you, a Joy."** Lulu Enterprises Incorporated, 22 Jun 2014. AZQuotes.com, Wind and Fly LTD, 2019. https://www.azquotes.com/quote/352796, accessed October 08, 2019.

Michael Beckwith, FaceBook post Sep 27, 2012 **"Don't look for your Dreams to become True; look to become True to Your Dreams."** https://www.facebook.com/Michael.B.Beckwith/photos/a.123452184784/10151182969309785/?type=3&theater

I have heard Rev. Michael say this in live trainings. Find out more about his work at https://agapelive.com/

Michael Beckwith has an amazing process called "*Life Visioning*". I highly recommend you try it. *Life Visioning: A Transformative Process for Activating Your Unique Gifts and Highest Potential.* Sounds True, 1 May 2013

Kahlil Gibran, *Sand and Foam, 1926* **"There must be something strangely sacred in salt. It is in our tears and in the sea."** Rajpal & Sons, 2012. AZQuotes.com, Wind and Fly LTD, 2019. https://www.azquotes.com/quote/718085, accessed October 08, 2019.

Robert Wyland, AZQuotes.com, Wind and Fly LTD, 2019. https://www.azquotes.com/quote/579929, accessed October 08, 2019. **"The ocean stirs the heart, inspires the imagination and brings eternal joy to the soul."**

Hakalau, description at NLP World. https://www.nlpworld.co.uk/nlp-glossary/h/hakalau/

Mark Anthony, post on instagram "And one day she discovered that she was fierce, and strong, and full of fire, and that not even she could hold herself back because her passion burned brighter than her fears."

https://www.instagram.com/markanthonypoet/?hl=en, from his book, *The Beautiful Truth*, CreateSpace Independent Publishing Platform, 10 Aug 2016, https://www.goodreads.com/quotes/9128902-and-one-day-she-discovered-that-she-was-fierce-and His latest books are on Amazon at amazon.com/author/markanthonypoet *Love Notes*, CreateSpace Independent Publishing Platform, July 22, 2018. *True Love*, Independently published, September 09, 2019

"Your mind believes everything you tell it! Fill it with LOVE", this was initially inspired by Jasmine Star's instagram post, where she credits Jay Shetty for this reminder. **https://www.instagram.com/p/B084YsADHSR/**

Elyse Hope-Killoran, (M+D-R). I was told about this formula by Hugh Gilbert who credited Elyse with it.
http://choosingprosperity.com/about-elyse/
http://www.magicalmedicalmysterytour.com/

Lao Zi, **"Water is the softest thing, yet it can penetrate mountains and earth. This shows clearly the principle of softness overcoming hardness."** AZQuotes.com, Wind and Fly LTD, 2019. https://www.azquotes.com/quote/765889, accessed October 08, 2019.

Tosha Silver, *It's Not Your Money: How to Live Fully from Divine Abundance*, p.16 The Full Abundance Prayer. Originally printed by Hay House, Inc, 5 Feb 2019. You can order a beautiful print of the abundance prayer from her website https://toshasilver.com/ , https://toshasilver.com/products/change-me-prayer-poster-1 There is also an earlier version on her FB page 19, July 2016 https://www.facebook.com/toshasilver/posts/blessed-full-moon-in-capricornhey-all-id-temporarily-vanished-off-the-earth-for-/669088393244187/

Thich Nhat Hanh, AZQuotes.com, Wind and Fly LTD, 2019. https://www.azquotes.com/quote/380225, accessed October 08, 2019. **"Many people think excitement is happiness . . .But when you are excited, you are not peaceful. True happiness is based on peace."**

"Looking behind, I am filled with gratitude,looking forward, I am filled with vision, looking upwards I am filled with strength, looking within, I discover peace." Quero Apache Prayer (source unknown) https://spiritualcleansing.org/category/author-quotes/native-american-proverb/

Billy Chapata, twitter post 23 Aug 2016, https://twitter.com/iambrillyant/status/768302767249068032
"I no longer force things. What flows, flows. What crashes, crashes. I only have space and energy for things that are meant for me." follow him on twitter https://twitter.com/iambrillyant?lang=en, His books include *Chameleon Aura*, Andrews McMeel Publishing, 22 Jan 2019

Yung Pueblo, twitter May 18, 2016, https://yungpueblo.tumblr.com/post/144556734328
"Your healing lifts up the whole ocean of existence. When you heal we all heal."

Rumi, **"If Light is in your Heart, you will find your way home."** AZQuotes.com, Wind and Fly LTD, 2019. https://www.azquotes.com/quote/496998, accessed October 08, 2019.

Further Inspiration and Recommend Reading

I've read books by the following, attended live workshops and listened to them online.

Further Inspiration and recommended reading

Dr David Hamilton *The Five Side Effects of Kindness*
https://drdavidhamilton.com
Dr David Hamilton *It's The Thought That Counts:Why Mind over Matter Really Works*
Pila of Hawaii *The Secrets and Mysteries of Hawaii*
http://www.mysticalhawaii.com/
Harry Uhane Jim *Wise Secrets of Aloha* http://harryjimlomilomi.com/10385.html
Michael Bernard Beckwith *Life Visioning* book and the online course https://www.michaelbernardbeckwith.com/
Michael Bernard Beckwith *Spiritual Liberation*
https://www.michaelbernardbeckwith.com/
Marianne Williamson *Return to Love* https://marianne.com
Marianne Williamson
http://www.oprah.com/spirit/marianne-williamson-what-you-think-is-what-you-get
Tosha Silver *It's Not Your Money*
Don Miguel Ruiz *The Four Agreements* https://www.miguelruiz.com

Joe Dispenza *Zero Limits* https://drjoedispenza.com/

Robert Holden *Success Intelligence* https://www.robertholden.com

Wayne Dyer *The Power of Intention* and I have heard him speak
https://www.drwaynedyer.com/

Sharon Blackie *If Women Rose Rooted* https://sharonblackie.net

Byron Katie *Your Inner Awakening* https://thework.com/

Hugh Gilbert *Free the Unicorn* http://www.hughgilbertauthor.com and
https://www.kineticchainrelease.com/our-team/hugh-gilbert/

Debbie Ford *The Dark Side of the Light Chasers: Reclaiming Your Power,
Creativity, Brilliance, and Dreams* https://www.debbieford.com

Michael A. Singer *The Untethered Soul* https://untetheredsoul.com

Mike Dooley *Infinite Possibilities: The Art of Living Your Dreams*
https://www.tut.com

Michael Neill *The Inside-Out Revolution* https://www.michaelneill.org

Eckhart Tolle *The Power of Now* https://www.eckharttolle.com

Matt Kahn *Whatever Arises Love That* https://mattkahn.org

Esther Hicks *Ask and it is Given* https://www.abraham-hicks.com

Rima Morrell *The Sacred Power of Huna: Spirituality and Shamanism in
Hawai'i*
https://www.simonandschuster.co.uk/authors/Rima-A-Morrell/460365901
https://www.innertraditions.com/books/the-sacred-power-of-huna

Rebecca Campbell *Light is the New Black* https://rebeccacampbell.me

Ali Campbell *Just Get on With It* https://alicampbell.com

Mastin Kipp *Daily Love* https://mastinkipp.com

Kyle Gray *Raise Your Vibration* https://www.kylegray.co.uk

Gabrielle Bernstein *The Universe Has Your Back*
https://gabbybernstein.com

Inspiring Films

What the Bleep do we know, https://whatthebleep.com
E-motion, https://www.e-motionthemovie.com

There are BONUS materials available on my website for you to download, including meditations, PDF's, journal prompts and more. I will continue to add to this over time as I am inspired to create more.
https://ionarussell.com/making-waves-bonus-material/

Making Waves

Lightning Source UK Ltd.
Milton Keynes UK
UKHW021903270220
359459UK00008B/234